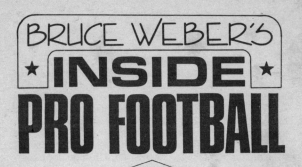

BRUCE WEBER'S
★ INSIDE ★
PRO FOOTBALL

1992

SCHOLASTIC INC.

New York Toronto London Auckland Sydney

PHOTO CREDITS

Cover: Photo of Mark Rypien © Bob Ewell/Sportschrome East/West. **vi, 6, 21, 58:** Washington Redskins. **2, 60:** Dallas Cowboys. **3, 78:** San Francisco 49ers. **4, 24, 30:** New England Patriots. **5, 76:** Atlanta Falcons. **7, 9, 20, 36:** Houston Oilers. **8, 22, 46:** Los Angeles Raiders. **10, 12, 26:** Buffalo Bills. **11, 54, 68:** Detroit Lions. **13, 14, 15, 56:** Philadelphia Eagles. **16, 18, 80:** New Orleans Saints. **17, 44:** Kansas City Chiefs. **19, 66, 84:** Chicago Bears. **23, 48:** Denver Broncos. **28:** New York Jets. **32:** Miami Dolphins. **34:** Indianapolis Colts. **38:** Cleveland Browns. **40:** Pittsburgh Steelers. **42:** Cincinnati Bengals. **50:** San Diego Chargers. **52:** Seattle Seahawks. **62:** New York Giants. **64:** Phoenix Cardinals. **70:** Tampa Bay Buccaneers. **72:** Minnesota Vikings. **74:** Green Bay Packers. **82:** Los Angeles Rams.

No part of this publication may be reproduced in whole or in part, or stored in a retrieval system, or transmitted in any form or by any means, electronic, mechanical, photocopying, recording, or otherwise, without written permission of the publisher. For information regarding permission, write to Scholastic Inc., 730 Broadway, New York, NY 10003.

ISBN 0-590-45626-1

Copyright © 1992 by Scholastic Inc.
All rights reserved. Published by Scholastic Inc.

12 11 10 9 8 7 6 5 4 3 2 1   2 3 4 5 6/9

Printed in the U.S.A.   01

First Scholastic printing, September 1992

CONTENTS

INTRODUCTION:
The Year of the Coach

If the 1992 NFL head coaches ever get together for a group picture, they'll have to wear name tags. Of the nine — count 'em — nine new coaches in the league, five are getting their first taste of action as field bosses, an incredibly high number. What about the other 19 field leaders? Will they still be around after 1992? Since coaches are hired to be fired, some probably won't.

Most of the new men trace their roots to the two most recent coaching legends, former 49er leader Bill Walsh and Miami's Don Shula. One, Cincinnati's David Shula, even carries the master's genes.

The NFC Central leads the pack of new faces. Three of the five teams open the season with first-year coaches, all out of the Walsh school. Tampa Bay's Sam Wyche was unemployed for only a week or two after the Cincinnati Bengals asked him to leave. Minnesota's Dennis Green arrives from Stanford, where he was the head coach. And Green Bay boss Mike Holmgren gets his first head-coaching job after years directing the potent 49er offense.

The only other NFC newcomer is the Rams' Chuck Knox — and he's not really a newcomer. The nine-year Seahawk coach returns to the Rams, scene of his greatest years (five NFC West titles in five seasons).

The 1991 group returns in the NFC East,

but the Giants' Ray Handley and the Cards' Joe Bugel are both on the hot seat. Bugel needs to win early; Giants fans expect no less than a play-off invitation in the league's toughest division.

Two first-time head coaches lead a 50% turnover in the AFC Central. Many Cincinnati fans believe that David Shula is no Don Shula, at least not yet. Pittsburgh shocked fans by picking Bill Cowher.

The AFC West lineup is a mix of old and new. Veteran college coach Bobby Ross gets his first pro shot (he has been an assistant) with San Diego. He runs an imaginative offense, just what the Chargers need. Seattle's Tom Flores owns the NFL's most unusual title, president-head coach of the Seahawks. Owner Ken Behring is looking for a better than 8–8 mark. In some places, the Raiders' Art Shell would be in jeopardy. But in L.A., where owner Al Davis stresses "family" along with pride and poise, Shell should survive.

Like Knox, Ted Marchibroda returns to a former location, as head coach of the Colts. Unlike Knox, the longtime Bills offensive coordinator would like to forget his first tour of duty with the club.

With nine new head coaches, chances are this should be a stable year for employment. But with millions of dollars on the line, who knows what drives owners nuts — and coaches to the unemployment line.

— Bruce Weber
April 1992

Cover Story
MARK RYPIEN
WASHINGTON REDSKINS

After the Washington Redskins ripped the Denver Broncos in Super Bowl XXII in January 1988, everyone expected the 'Skins would be back soon. But it took until January 1992, mainly because no one stepped up to run the offense until then. Washington insiders (football variety) always figured Mark Rypien would be the man.

Injuries sidelined the Washington State U. star for most of two seasons, leaving Redskin boss Joe Gibbs to search for the quarterback of the future. When the future arrived, however, it was Rypien.

Protected by football's best offensive line and with Washington's outstanding receivers group, Rypien finally showed what he could do last season. Mark wound up with 249 completions on 421 passes, a 59.1% accuracy rate. His 28 TD tosses were second only to Buffalo's Jim Kelly, and his QB rating of 97.9 ranked only behind San Francisco's Steve Young (101.8).

Selected as the NFC's Pro Bowl starter, Rypien led Washington to play-off wins over Atlanta (24–7) and Detroit (41–10), before hitting 18 of 33 for 292 yards and two TDs in the Super Bowl rout of Buffalo. The only question about Rypien: How much money would Washington be willing to pay him?

National Football League All-Pro Team

Wide Receiver
MICHAEL IRVIN
DALLAS COWBOYS

When the Dallas Cowboys made Michael Irvin their first draft pick (the 11th choice overall) in 1988, the Miami (FL) U. wide receiver thought pro football would be like college ball: all fun, games, and success. It is now, but it took a while.

For his first 2½ pro seasons, Irvin felt trapped. Injuries, including a serious ligament tear, kept him on the sidelines much of the time. And the Cowboys were awful. But Irvin's return to good health, the arrival of QB Troy Aikman, and the turnaround engineered by his old college coach, Jimmy Johnson, changed all that.

In '91 Irvin and his teammates put it all together. A healthy Michael caught everything in sight, led the NFC (and finished second in the NFL) with 93 catches for 1,523 yards (tops in the league by 183 yards), and caught eight TDs. He practically rewrote the Cowboys' receiving record book with seven 100-yard games (including a record-tying three straight) and team marks for yardage and catches. And only two years after going 1–15, the Cowboys went 11–5 and returned to the NFL play-offs.

"When he's healthy, Michael can make the plays," says coach Johnson. "I think his '91 performance proves that."

Wide Receiver
JERRY RICE
SAN FRANCISCO 49ERS

Steve Young, who came to the San Francisco 49ers camp last summer expecting to back up Joe Montana again, wound up the '91 season as the NFL's top-rated quarterback. Young will be the first to tell you that having Jerry Rice out wide will help you become the NFL's top-rated QB.

Despite the Niners' struggle (they lost six of their first ten and missed the play-offs for the first time since 1982), Rice maintained his place on our All-Pro team. There was competition, of course, from Andre Reed, Haywood Jeffires, and his All-Pro opposite number, Michael Irvin. But if you were starting a new club and had your choice of any wide receiver in the league, you'd probably start with the 6–2, 200-pound San Francisco flyer.

Starting his eighth NFL season after a storied career at tiny Mississippi Valley State, Rice hasn't lost a thing. He is still quick, catches the ball over the middle, and runs and runs after making the catch.

That's how Rice passed Dwight Clark and Roger Craig last season to become the Niners' all-time receiving leader with 525 catches. His 80 grabs in '91 ranked third in the NFC, and his 1,206 yards marked his sixth straight year with over 1,000.

Tight End
MARV COOK
NEW ENGLAND PATRIOTS

Look at the New England Patriots receiving corps and you think coach Dick MacPherson got it right out of the kitchen. With a Cook and a Fryar, you have everything you need for a feast except a microwave. Coach Mac is working on it.

Irving Fryar has been a household word in New England for years. But for Pro Bowler Cook, his new-found fame is extremely satisfying. A 1989 third-round draft pick from Iowa, the 6–4, 234-pound Cook has always caught the ball with the NFL's top tight ends. But with the arrival of MacPherson and his new staff, Cook became a vital part of the Patriots offense.

"I quickly saw Marv as a Pete Holohan-type of receiver," says new offensive coordinator Dick Coury, who coached Holohan with the L.A. Rams. Good company, but Cook proved he was even better. His 82 catches for 808 yards were 23 better than Holohan's best year and only two shy of the Pats' all-time record (84 by Stanley Morgan in 1986).

"Marv knows the game," says quarterback Hugh Millen. "He takes a lot of shots from linebackers over the middle. Then he just dusts himself off and gets ready to do it again."

Offensive Tackle
MIKE
KENN
ATLANTA FALCONS

The Atlanta Falcons had been down so long, they didn't even know which way was up. And while it took a package of new faces to help the Birds turn the corner, veteran tackle Mike Kenn led the resurgence.

Fact is, some of the modern-day Falcons were in grade school when Kenn started his long Atlanta career. When opening day rolls around in '92, the 6–7, 280-pound Kenn will be starting his 15th NFL campaign. Mike has started 200-plus NFL games, more than some of his teammates have *seen!*

But like cheese and fine wine and numerous other classics that get better with age, so does Mike. The one-time Michigan Wolverine allowed just one quarterback sack on the 531 pass plays that were run while he was in there last season. Overall, with Kenn partnered with another Pro Bowler, Chris Hinton, the Falcons permitted only one sack in every 17 attempts, the best in club history. The line also blocked for the NFC's fifth best running game. With balance on offense and defense, Atlanta got as far as the NFC finals against eventual Super Bowl champ Washington.

With the team moving to the new Georgia Dome this fall, Mike Kenn is expecting big things in 1992.

Offensive Tackle
JIM LACHEY
WASHINGTON REDSKINS

The casual Redskins fan thinks his or her team reigns as world champions because Mark Rypien is the NFL's best passer or the Redskins defense is manned by 11 Supermen or Chip Lohmiller can kick the ball out of any park except Yellowstone.

Insiders know, however, that it's the 'Skins offensive line that drives the Washington scoring machine and that Jim Lachey is the major cog in the machine.

We can say it without any doubt: Jim Lachey is the best left tackle in football and maybe the best in a long, long time. His opponents know how good the 6–6, 294-pounder is: He has been the NFC's starter at LT in each of the last two Pro Bowls.

A one-time San Diego Charger and, briefly, a Los Angeles Raider, the 29-year-old Lachey enjoyed a practically perfect '91 season. Playing against the NFL's best, he allowed exactly zero sacks. In fact, the entire 'Skins line permitted only a league-low nine sacks (just about a half-a-sack per game) all season. In addition, Washington had the NFL's seventh-ranked rushing game, with a staff of running backs that didn't scare most of the league.

As Washington continues to reshape the old Hogs, Jim Lachey will be the key.

Guard
MIKE MUNCHAK
HOUSTON OILERS

It was no accident that the Houston Oilers offensive line was rated among the NFL's best in 1991. Its anchor, left guard Mike Munchak, earned his seventh Pro Bowl trip, just one behind the club record set by Elvin Bethea. At age 32, Munchak should tie Bethea early next February.

Munchak, a 10-year veteran from Penn State, scored his postseason honors (which included AP All-Pro first-team selection) last season despite missing three Oiler outings with a knee injury. That's how much respect his rivals have for Munchak. In fact, Oiler teammates call him Canton, referring to his next stop, the Pro Football Hall of Fame.

"I haven't even thought about it," says the 6–3, 284-pound Munchak. "Whenever anyone else has brought it up, I always believe they're joking. The Hall of Fame isn't something you think about when you're playing. You only think about it after you retire."

Retirement isn't foremost on Mike's mind these days. With his leadership, the Oiler line ranked second in the NFL in percentage of sacks allowed and second in the AFC in total sacks allowed. "I want to play at least two more years," he says, "and I want to play in a Super Bowl."

Guard
STEVE WISNIEWSKI
LOS ANGELES RAIDERS

Starting only his fourth NFL season, Steve Wisniewski of the Raiders owns just about every honor in the game — except a Super Bowl ring. "That's one of my dreams," says the 6–4, 280-pound left guard.

A year ago, this profile would have read right guard. But when the Raiders picked up veteran right guard Max Montoya via Plan B from the Bengals in 1991, they asked Wisniewski to shift to the left. "It was like a right-handed person trying to write left-handed," Wisniewski said early last year. But he got the hang of it quickly. A Pro Bowler on the right side in 1990, only his sophomore season, Steve made his second straight trip in '91.

"I didn't mind making the switch," the one-time Penn State star said. "Max has been a real inspiration to me. I learn something new from him every day."

Wisniewski was the Raiders' initial pick in the '89 draft. L.A. traded up to get Steve as the first selection in the second round. (They didn't have a pick in the first round.)

The 25-year-old brother of former Colt lineman Leo Wisniewski, Steve figures to be an All-Pro for another decade. By that time, he could well own that Super Bowl ring.

Center
BRUCE MATTHEWS
HOUSTON OILERS

The NFL's best center never wanted to play center. "The last thing you want to do in your career is change positions," said Matthews last year. After all, he'd been a Pro Bowl guard for three years and was rated as one of the game's best. But when the Houston Oilers needed an emergency center in 1990, they turned to their star right guard. It wasn't long before the coaches loved what they saw.

"It looked like Doug Dawson would be our center last season," said Matthews, who split time between guard and center at training camp. But when Dawson went down with a preseason knee injury, Matthews became the main man.

How could an All-Pro guard become an All-Pro center overnight? "I don't know many players who could make the switch successfully," said teammate Mike Munchak, himself an All-Pro left guard. "But Bruce is so smart. And the major change is mental. The center makes the calls, and we live or die by his judgment."

Mostly they live. The Oilers offensive line is a key to their success, and their new man in the middle drives the line.

Bruce has one disappointment. He hasn't played in a Super Bowl. Maybe this year!

Quarterback
JIM
KELLY
BUFFALO BILLS

Maybe Jim Kelly ought to ask for a salary cut. He just doesn't work hard enough. With the Buffalo Bills no-huddle offense and great targets like Andre Reed and Thurman Thomas, Kelly frequently gets the Bills down the field and into the end zone quicker than a hot dog vendor can splash on the mustard.

Though Kelly, Buffalo's most eligible bachelor, took much of the heat when the Washington Redskins ended the Bills season on a Super Bowl down note last January, insiders point to a porous Buffalo offensive line as the cause of the problem. The 31-year-old Kelly, who turned the University of Miami program around a decade ago, had another super season. He completed 304 of 474 passes (64.1%) for 3,844 yards and 33 touchdowns in 15 starts.

The Bills players are thrilled with the results of their no-huddle offense and Kelly's leadership. "I love it," says Jim, "because I'm doing what every quarterback would love to do: call his own plays. It changes how I prepare for a game, of course. I'm always looking for keys, the things the defense will let us do. But it's great to be able to call the plays, dictate the routes, the whole thing."

10

BARRY SANDERS
DETROIT LIONS

The image of the flashy NFL running back ends with Barry Sanders. There's no jiving, no hot-dogging, no ego-tripping. The word so many use to describe Sanders is *humble*. And it fits.

Nothing could make Detroit Lions coach Wayne Fontes any happier — except dropping the Washington Redskins from the NFL! "At the start of last season," says the 1991 NFL coach of the year, "I told everyone we had to get the ball into Barry's hands. So our opponents squeezed the line of scrimmage. They couldn't stop Sanders, of course, and it opened up the offense."

For the first time in anyone's memory (it was 1983, actually), the Lions qualified for the play-offs, establishing a franchise record with 12 victories. And Sanders was in the middle of everything. With eight 100-yard rushing performances, Barry became the first Lion — and only the seventh NFL player — ever with 1,000 yards or more in each of his first three seasons. In a key road victory over the Vikings, he enjoyed Detroit's first ever 200-yard game (220 actual) while rushing for a team-record four TDs.

Barry may be humble, but others around him aren't. As his father, William, says, "Barry is the best!"

Running Back
THURMAN THOMAS
BUFFALO BILLS

When his chance at revenge finally came, Thurman Thomas blew it. The Buffalo Bills' versatile running back thought he was robbed of the MVP award at Super Bowl XXV, when his team lost to the New York Giants, 20–19. He was probably right. So when the Bills qualified for another Super shot last January, Thomas announced that he would right the previous wrong by dominating the big game.

It never happened. Thomas couldn't find his helmet after the opening kickoff, missed the first two plays, and never really got untracked. He wound up with only 13 yards on 10 carries — and blamed teammates.

What a terrible way to end a great season. The 5–10, 198-pound Thomas had his best season in '91, with 1,407 yards rushing and another 631 on passes, becoming only the 11th player in NFL history to gain more than 2,000 combined yards from scrimmage. He also led the AFC in rushing and tied for the conference lead in touchdowns with an even dozen.

How important is Thomas, a one-time college teammate of Detroit's All-Pro RB Barry Sanders? Thomas has rushed for 100 or more yards in 20 regular-season games. The Bills record in those contests: 20–0!

Defensive End
REGGIE WHITE
PHILADELPHIA EAGLES

When you are the leader of a defense that finishes first against the run, first against the pass, and first in total defense, you must be doing something right.

DE Reggie White does plenty right. That's why he's our All-Pro defensive end and why his linemates are All-Pros, too.

Starting his eighth NFL season, the Minister of Defense, as White is called, is the most feared defender in the league. Opponents double- and triple-team him, yet he still leads his team in sacks (15, second in the NFL) and QB hurries.

Off the field, White is possibly the most peaceful man in football. He's an ordained minister and devotes most of his free time to doing good. On the field, it's a different story. White is a monster. The future Hall-of-Famer now has made 110 sacks in 105 games, the leading figure over the last seven seasons. He was in on 98 tackles, 68 of them solos in '91. Though Reggie usually lines up at left end, opponents are likely to find him anywhere on the field.

"When Bud Carson came on as defensive coordinator last season, he gave me more freedom," says Reggie. "Now I can set up anywhere and do anything." Eagle opponents didn't need more to worry about.

13

Defensive End
CLYDE SIMMONS
PHILADELPHIA EAGLES

In Philadelphia the "other" defensive end struggles for recognition. High-profile, outspoken Reggie White gets most of the ink. But football insiders concede that the quiet Clyde Simmons is just as powerful on the other side. And when Simmons was voted to the NFC Pro Bowl team last year, his Eagle teammates had only one comment: "It's about time!"

Off the field, the 6–6, 275-pound Simmons doesn't say much. On the field, it's different. "It's amazing," says teammate Seth Joyner. "Clyde is a pussycat in the locker room and a lion once the whistle blows."

"None of us will go near Clyde when he's mad," says teammate Jerome Brown. "If he's getting on an official or an opponent, you just stay away until he cools off."

In those rare moments when he's willing to talk, Simmons will talk only about football and never about himself. "I take this very seriously," he says. "I used to have more fun. But it's a business, and you get ready like your life depends upon it."

Although he claims he was better in 1989, Simmons was outstanding in '91. (He missed the entire preseason in a contract dispute.) His 13½ sacks ranked second on the Eagles to White (15).

Defensive Tackle
JEROME BROWN
PHILADELPHIA EAGLES

When the Philadelphia Eagles plucked Jerome Brown off the U. of Miami roster in the first round of the 1987 NFL draft, they figured they had a defensive tackle for a decade. They didn't figure that Brown would let his weight balloon up (330 or more?), that nagging injuries would handicap his progress, or that his big mouth would be more powerful than his on-field performance.

That all ended in 1991. "I finally got control of myself," says Brown. "I had been partying very hard, and my weight was out of control. I had to do something about it."

NFL backs paid the price. As the Eagles led the league in defense — rushing, passing, and total — in '91, it was Brown getting the job done. Always a premier run-stuffer, Jerome was equally punishing on the pass, drawing double-team blocking, allowing teammates to work one-on-one, and racking up nine sacks. He also wound up with 133 tackles, 81 of them solos. No other Eagle lineman did as much.

"I also learned to play with pain," says Brown. "Before, when I got nicked up, I'd sit out. People got the wrong idea about me and I didn't like it. Now, I'm going to take care of myself all year round."

Outside Linebacker
PAT SWILLING
NEW ORLEANS SAINTS

As sportswriters search the grass (or AstroTurf) for the next Lawrence Taylor, they don't have to look much past Pat Swilling. There are some votes for Philly's Seth Joyner and Buffalo's Cornelius Bennett. But to most experts, it's either Kansas City's Derrick Thomas or Swilling for the next half decade or so.

That's why New Orleans Saints fans were so upset when Swilling, a six-year veteran, signed an offer sheet with the Detroit Lions this spring and were relieved when the Saints matched the offer. Having just about the best set of linebackers in the game, the Saints need Swilling for their ferocious pass-rush.

"I work hard at rushing the passer," says Swilling, the 1991 NFL leader with 17 sacks (for a career total of 66 in six seasons). "But it's worth it. I live for the sack." In fact, during one memorable five-game stretch last season, Pat rang up 10½ sacks and forced four fumbles. No one has ever wrecked more offenses so often for so long.

Swilling's furious pass-rush has earned him enormous respect, some of which Pat can do without. "Last year Atlanta kept Andre Rison in eight times to help Mike Kenn block me. And Kenn's an All-Pro!"

16

Outside Linebacker
DERRICK THOMAS
KANSAS CITY CHIEFS

Try to talk football with Kansas City's Derrick Thomas and you'll find that he's more interested in Third and Long. Not the down and distance where the Alabama grad terrorizes the AFC; Thomas's Third and Long is a nifty new reading program that helps 58 youngsters in the Kansas City area. The 58 figure is no accident; Thomas wears No. 58 while he flattens enemy quarterbacks.

The 6–3, 236-pound, superquick Thomas spends Saturdays before Chiefs home games in a local library, reading stories to the young people and lending a sympathetic ear to help with their problems. Third and Long also sponsors summer camps, tutoring sessions, a summer basketball league, and a festive Christmas party.

On Sundays, however, Thomas is kind to absolutely no one. After a slow start, produced by opponents focusing their blocking plans on Derrick, he wound up second in the AFC with 13½ sacks along with 79 tackles (60 solos).

The fourth overall pick of the 1989 NFL draft (Troy Aikman, Tony Mandarich, and Barry Sanders were chosen ahead of him), Thomas's Pro Bowl record (three years, three invitations) remains perfect.

17

Inside Linebacker
SAM
MILLS
NEW ORLEANS SAINTS

If good things come in small packages, then New Orleans inside linebacker Sam Mills should be an All-Pro every year. Playing at a position where most standouts would qualify as NBA forwards, Mills reminds you of another sport: bowling. At 5–9 and 225 pounds, Sam is a round mound of power who loves to put his helmet square on the chest of rival blockers.

Sam arrived with the Saints almost accidentally. Cut by the Cleveland Browns after a stellar career at Montclair (NJ) State, he figured his football days were over. In fact, he was teaching photography and woodworking at East Orange (NJ) High School when the United States Football League was born in 1982. He hooked up with the Philadelphia Stars and led the team in tackles three straight years. That message wasn't lost on Stars coach Jim Mora, who became the head Saint.

Sam was on the verge of signing with the Bears, whose defensive leader was too-short Mike Singletary, when he spent one day at the Saints camp. He never left.

A Pro Bowler in 1987 and '88, Sam rejects the too-small image. "Forget the 5–9 stuff," says longtime teammate Pat Swilling. "Sam just plays with heart."

Inside Linebacker
MIKE SINGLETARY
CHICAGO BEARS

We have this thing about Mike Single-tary. We love the guy. Last year we announced in this space that 1991 would be Mike's last year in the middle of the Chicago Bears defense. He said it; we believed it. So we named him to our All-Pro team, as usual, figuring that the toughest gentle man in the NFL would go out on top. He had another super season. Then, on the day the Bears lost to Dallas in the NFC play-offs, Mike announced that he'd be back in 1992. So here he is again, on our All-Pro team.

"I see some great things coming with this team," he said, "and I think I can contribute." He sure can! At age 33, the fireplug-sized Singletary (6–0, 230) admits that 1991, his 11th pro season, was a good one. His 124 tackles led the team (by 27); for the last 10 seasons, he has ranked first or second among the Bears in that department.

Then there was the shot he dished out to Green Bay's Ed West that broke the Packer's steel face mask. It blew the minds of everyone who loves Bears football. To the humble Singletary, however, "it was probably a faulty face mask."

So here's Singletary again and, if he decides to play in 1993, he'll probably be our All-Pro choice again.

Cornerback
CRIS DISHMAN
HOUSTON OILERS

Oilers coach Jack Pardee sees Cris Dishman make another great play, and he smiles. Not that an interception, a fumble recovery, or a strip wouldn't please any head coach. But his pleasure is extra special because two years ago, Dishman was on the way to self-destructing.

"He was out of control," says Pardee. "When Jerry Glanville was coaching here, he loved Cris's bad-guy image and called him half crazy. But Cris would do things that would hurt himself — and the team."

Once, in a 1990 preseason game in Minnesota, he intercepted a Viking pass and headed for the end zone. But he started dancing at the five-yard line and dropped the ball, costing the Oilers a touchdown. He'd bark at injured opponents and talk trash to anyone within hearing range.

The arrival of the low-key Pardee — and Cris's marriage to Karen — changed all that. "My past was filled with controversy. People loved to hate me. Now that I'm making the plays and not doing crazy stuff, everyone is trying to get to know me."

And with good reason. Cris earned his first Pro Bowl invite with six interceptions, 23 passes defensed, three fumble recoveries, and 65 tackles.

Cornerback
DARRELL GREEN
WASHINGTON REDSKINS

To celebrate the Super Bowl in Minneapolis last January, the NFL set up a show for fans called "The NFL Experience." Visitors could try their hand at passing, kicking, or even matching strides with the NFL's fastest human, Darrell Green.

Green wasn't there, of course. He and his mates were preparing to rout the Buffalo Bills in another ho-hum final game. But a series of flashing lights on the wall depicted the Redskins cornerback's blazing speed. The NFL didn't report whether anyone caught the Washington speedster. But the light show clearly proved what NFL receivers have known for years: You can't run away from Darrell Green.

Starting his tenth season, the 5-8, 170-pound Green has won five Pro Bowl trips. He earned his latest Honolulu visit with five interceptions and 79 tackles (64 of them solos) in '91. He also defensed 21 passes to lead the 'Skins.

Darrell is especially tough under pressure. In a Monday night game against Philadelphia last year, he picked off a couple of Eagles passes. And his seven tackles and overtime interception enabled Washington to beat the high-flying Houston Oilers.

RONNIE LOTT

LOS ANGELES RAIDERS

The San Francisco 49ers haven't made many personnel mistakes. For years the Niners "won" their trades, hung on to their free agents, and picked the draft board clean. The result: Super Bowl victory after Super Bowl victory.

But when the 49ers left safety Ronnie Lott unprotected in the winter of '91, they committed the ultimate goof. Sure, Lott was banged up. Sure, Lott would be 32 by opening day. But the 6–0, 205-pounder was right up among the league leaders in hitting hard — and that's still the name of the game.

Lott quickly returned to his old college (Southern Cal) home, the L.A. Coliseum, with the Raiders. Instantly he proved that the 49ers had moved too soon.

The 1991 season was just another great Pro Bowl year for Lott. No other active player owns as many interceptions (59), as Ronnie and his eight pickoffs led the league in '91. Even better, he seemed to hit just as hard as ever. "If you hear a loud noise on the field," says nose tackle Bob Golic, "you know Ronnie is hitting someone."

"I had to learn a few things in the AFC," says Lott, "but once the ball is snapped, you just try to make things happen."

Free Safety
STEVE ATWATER
DENVER BRONCOS

By midseason last year, it was clear that three-year veteran Steve Atwater of the Denver Broncos was having his best season. Trouble was, nobody noticed. But as the Broncos continued their improbable comeback that left them just three points short of another Super Bowl trip, the people who know started identifying Atwater as one of Denver's defensive heroes.

Of course, the 6–3, 217-pounder has been the focus of attention everywhere he has gone. A first-round draft pick out of Arkansas in 1989, Atwater is three-for-three in Pro Bowl trips. But his All-Pro selection signals a new level for the superquick safety. It figured, however, after Atwater finished second on the Broncos in tackles (83 solos plus 67 assists for 150) and tied for first in interceptions (5).

Still, Atwater is pleased with the recognition he gets. "I was kind of shocked with a third Pro Bowl selection," he said. "I think I made some great plays, but I could have made more. But I'm extremely happy."

Why is Steve a regular on AFC All-Teams? According to one insider, "He has the ability to be both a tremendous hitter and a good coverage guy. You don't find that combination very often."

Tight end Marv Cook caught 82 passes, only two shy of the team record, in leading the New England Patriots' 1991 comeback.

American Football Conference Team Previews

AFC East
BUFFALO BILLS
1991 Finish: First
1992 Prediction: First

Cornelius Bennett

Andre Reed

It will take all the smarts coach Marv Levy owns to send the Buffalo Bills back for another Super Bowl visit next January. Last year's tour was a disaster: The no-huddle was useless, the offensive line was exposed, Thurman Thomas whined, and the Bills were embarrassed.

Another visit isn't out of the question, however. Jim Kelly (304 of 474, 3,844 yards, 33 TDs) is, arguably, the game's top QB, especially when he's in complete command of the offense. Frank Reich (6 TDs on only 27 completions) is a top backup.

Thomas, who'd like to forget Super Bowl week, is the NFL's most versatile back (288 carries for 1,407 yards and 7 TDs rushing, 62 catches for 631 yards and 5 TDs receiving). If Levy opts for more two-back sets,

FB Carwell Gardner (42 for 146, 4 TDs) will shine. There's good depth here, too.

Andre Reed (81 catches, 1,113 yards, 10 TDs) is one of the best, and, even at age 36, James Lofton (57 catches, 1,072 yards, 8 TDs) is still capable. There's strength at TE with Keith McKeller and Pete Metzelaars, though Butch Rolle was a Plan B loss.

After the Redskins loss, people began to raise questions about the Buffalo offensive line. Still, the Bills are relatively strong with tackles Howard Ballard and Will Wolford, guards Jim Ritcher and Glenn Parker, and center Kent Hull. Injured G John Davis will miss part of '92, and Ritcher is now 34. Top pick John Fina fits here.

The defensive line could present problems, unless DRE Bruce Smith's knee is 100%. NT Jeff Wright is good, if a bit small. DLE Leon Seals was unhappy this spring. Draftee James Patton may step up.

The linebackers are the heart of the defense, though LILB Shane Conlan seems to be injury-prone. Still, there's plenty of strength with OLBs Cornelius Bennett and Darryl Talley, who join ILB Carlton Bailey, the hero of the '91 AFC championship victory over Denver. Ex-Cowboy Darrick Brownlow and ex-Oiler Eric Fairs help.

Though the secondary was picked apart by Washington's Mark Rypien, it's adequate. The Bills still need a big, strong safety (Matt Darby?) to go with Leonard Smith and Mark Kelso. Nate Odomes and Kirby Jackson are the corners.

AFC East
NEW YORK JETS
1991 Finish: Second
1992 Prediction: Second

Jeff Lageman   **Al Toon**

The Jets try to improve upon their strange
'91 season that saw them win games they
should have lost and lose games they figured to win. Bottom line: 8–8 and a rare
play-off trip.

Does it get better? A definite maybe. New
York needs help at left tackle, outside linebacker, and tight end while preparing for
the future at quarterback. It won't be easy.

Coach Bruce Coslet would love to see
untested second-year QB Browning Nagle
take over from Ken O'Brien (287 of 489, 3,300
yards, only 11 TDs). O'Brien is smart, tough,
and probably not the guy to lead a team to
a Super Bowl. Third-stringer Troy Taylor's
arm isn't strong enough.

If RB Blair Thomas (189 carries, 789 yards,
3 TDs) recovers from a key confidence-kill-

ing fumble against Chicago in '91, the Jets will be in great shape. It's a big if; Thomas hasn't proven that he should have been a No. 2 draft pick. Bruising blocking FB Brad Baxter also scored an AFC-leading 11 TDs last year. He's wonderful. There's depth with aging vets Freeman McNeil (the Jets' all-time leading rusher) and Johnny Hector.

WRs Al Toon (74 catches, 963 yards, but no TDs) and Rob Moore (70, 987, 5 TDs) are fine, but the Jets need another burner outside. TE is a problem, though ex-Colt Pat Beach and top draft pick Johnny Mitchell may push Mark Boyer and Chris Dressel.

C Jim Sweeney and RT Irv Eatman lead a so-so offensive line that could use a replacement for LT Jeff Criswell.

DRE Jeff Lageman has finally proved why he was a first-round draft pick. LE Marvin Washington and tackles Scott Mersereau and Dennis Byrd are better than adequate. MLB Kyle Clifton is first-rate, joining '91's super rookie Mo Lewis on the left, with No. 2 draft Kurt Barber and so-so Joe Kelly on the right.

The secondary will be improved if LCB Tony Stargell can recover his rookie-year form. He lost his starting job to Mike Brim, who joined James Hasty on the corners. FS Lonnie Young was superb after coming over from Phoenix, and SS Brian Washington got the job done most of the time.

Ancient PK Pat Leahy may not recover from back troubles, opening the way for Raul Allegre or Jason Staurovsky.

AFC East
NEW ENGLAND PATRIOTS
1991 Finish: Fourth
1992 Prediction: Third

Vincent Brown   Leonard Russell

The '92 season will provide a major test of character for the New England Patriots. Built through some sage drafting, the Pats bounced back from a horrid 1–15 season in '90 to go 6–10 under 61-year-old rookie head coach Dick MacPherson in '91. The Cowboys went from 1–15 to the play-offs in only two seasons. Can the Pats do the same?

Perhaps. QB Hugh Millen (246 of 409, 3,073 yards, 9 TDs) stepped up as the new QB of the future in Foxboro, MA. But some experts still have doubts about this six-year man. Tommy Hodson (36 of 68, 345 yards, one TD) is on hand.

RB Leonard Russell, the Pats' No. 2 draft pick a year ago, was better than anyone expected. The AFC Offensive Rookie of the Year picked up 959 yards on 266 carries. He should pair well with John Stephens (63 for 163), with Jon Vaughn in a support role.

All-Pro TE Marv Cook (82 catches, 808 yards, 3 TDs) is a top possession receiver, but the WR situation depends on the status of Hart Lee Dykes, who missed all of '91. Greg McMurtry (41 catches, 614 yards, 2 TDs) and 10-year vet Irving Fryar (68 catches, 1,014 yards, 3 TDs) should get the call in any event. Overall, it's a solid group.

The offensive line is a mixed bag. The tackles, vet Bruce Armstrong and '91 top pick Pat Harlow, are excellent. There will be changes at guard, with newcomer Reggie Redding, Calvin Stephens, and top '92 pick Eugene Chung looking to take over. Gene Chilton should be back at center, while the Pats take a good look at Plan Bs Scott Bowles and Larry Williams.

Similarly, the defensive front is adequate, though it lacks a big pass-rusher. Ray Agnew and Brent Williams hold down the ends, with Tim Goad in the middle.

The linebacker group keys the entire defense. When the Pats play a 3–4, Andre Tippett and Chris Singleton should work outside, with Eugene Lockhart and Vincent Brown, New England's best defensive player in '91, on the inside.

The secondary is the biggest problem. CB Maurice Hurst is outstanding, and '91 rookie Jerome Henderson is coming. But the remaining starters, CB Ronnie Lippett and S Fred Marion survived Plan B. Rookie Rod Smith could start.

AFC East
MIAMI DOLPHINS
1991 Finish: Third
1992 Prediction: Fourth

Louis Oliver

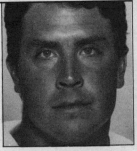

Dan Marino

We've heard this song before: For the Miami Dolphins to become an AFC East power again, they need defense, defense, defense. Coach Don Shula, only the second 300-game winner in NFC coaching history, was embarrassed by his team in '91. When a victory in either of the final two games would have clinched a play-off berth, the Fish blew them both.

Dan Marino (318 of 549, 3,970 yards, 25 TDs) remains one of the NFL's premier franchise quarterbacks. Marino videos should be required viewing for any young passer. Backups Scott Secules and Scott Mitchell are first-rate; one may be traded.

Mark Duper (at age 33) and Mark Clayton (at age 31) continue to provide great targets for Marino. Each caught 70 passes in '91, and each picked up more than 1,000 yards, though Clayton won the TD battle, 12–5. They'll need a young, fast backup soon; Tony Martin isn't the guy. TE Ferrell Edmonds should be the guy; he just doesn't do it every Sunday.

The running game remains a major hangup because big, fast, talented Sammie Smith didn't become the back everyone thought he'd be and was traded to Denver for RB Bobby Humphrey. Mark Higgs, with less talent, picked up 905 yards on 231 carries. FB Tony Paige is excellent but will be pressed by Plan B James Saxon.

The front five is good enough, especially on pass protection, with LT Richmond Webb and RG Harry Galbreath the leaders. C Jeff Uhlenhake and RT Mark Dennis are a little weak on the run.

The defensive line is *really* weak on the run, as in helpless. Ends T.J. Turner and Jeff Cross didn't get it done on the pass-rush, either. Rookie Larry Webster might help. Linebacking is questionable, too, especially if RILB John Offerdahl doesn't rebound after knee surgery. Though RILB Mike Reichenbach left for San Francisco, LOLB David Griggs, ROLB Bryan Cox, and LILB Cliff Odom should be back, and draftee Marco Coleman should fit.

In the secondary, safeties Bobby Harden and Louis Oliver are excellent. The corners, Vestee Jackson and J.B. Brown, aren't. Look for Plan B CB Bruce Alexander and top pick Troy Vincent to challenge.

33

AFC East
INDIANAPOLIS COLTS
1991 Finish: Fifth
1992 Prediction: Fifth

Jeff George

Jeff Herrod

Would you write a life insurance policy on Indianapolis QB Jeff George? You'd have to give it lots of thought. The Colts' franchise QB was sacked 56 times and knocked down even more often in '91. How long can he take a licking and keep on ticking?

The offensive line was the major problem. Lack of talent and an incredible run of injuries robbed the front five of any chance to click. Indy used 15 different players at these spots in '91. One-time Colt All-Pro G Ron Solt is back (Plan B) from Philly, but he's not what he once was. A healthy C Ray Donaldson and LT Irv Pankey would help. C Trevor Matich arrives, too, but mostly as a long-snapper. That's important. The Colts punted 82 times last year.

If he lives, the immobile George (292 of 485, 2,910 yards, 10 TDs) is one of the best. Injury-prone Jack Trudeau will back up, with Tom Tupa and Mark Herrmann battling for No. 3. Having new coach Ted Marchibroda on hand will help them all.

Any coach would love to have WR Bill Brooks (72 catches, 888 yards, 4 TDs), the Colts' top offensive performer in '91. Reggie Langhorne comes from Cleveland to join Brooks and Jessie Hester (60 catches, 753 yards, 5 TDs).

You figure the Colts running backs. Eric Dickerson (167 carries, 536 yards) is gone. Albert Bentley tries to come back from knee surgery at 33. Anthony Johnson is decent enough when he's healthy. And little (5–9) Ken Clark (114 carries, 366 yards) is OK.

With proper drafting, the Colts defensive front is OK, though ends Jon Hand and Donnell Thompson (injured knee) are getting on in years. Tony Siragusa should get the call at DT, joining the NFL's top pick, Steve Entman, who should be a star soon. The linebackers are decent, and Duane Bickett and Jeff Herrod are better than that. The No. 2 pick, Quentin Coryatt, and Plan B Carl Zander could help instantly.

The secondary is at least two players short. John Baylor, Keith Taylor, and Mike Prior were at the safeties in '91 and could be back in '92. Chris Goode and Eugene Daniel again man the corners. Rookie Ashley Ambrose is excellent on man-coverage.

AFC Central
HOUSTON OILERS
1991 Finish: First
1992 Prediction: First

Warren Moon

Haywood Jeffires

Trying to figure out the Houston Oilers is like coming up with the answers on one of those ink-blot tests psychiatrists like. You can't do it. The team has talent (eight Pro Bowlers), a relatively easy division, one of the NFL's best defenses, and a high-powered offense that's made to order for these players. But Houston remains one of nine teams never to visit the Super Bowl, and, though they have a real shot this year, you don't feel comfortable picking them.

QB Warren Moon (404 of 655, 4,690 yards, 23 TDs) became only the second man ever to put together back-to-back 4,000-yard seasons. On the down side, he fired 21 interceptions. The Oilers will dip badly if backup Cody Carlson is forced to play.

Losing slot receiver Drew Hill (90 catches,

1,109 yards, 4 TDs) via Plan B to Atlanta is a major problem. WRs Tony Jones and Alex Johnson left, too. But Haywood Jeffires (100 catches, 1,181 yards, 7 TDs) is back, along with Ernest Givins (70 catches, 996 yards, 5 TDs), Curtis Duncan (55 catches, 588 yards, 4 TDs), and Hill's backup, Leonard Harris. Ex-Packer Jeff Query should help.

Though Houston's run-and-shoot attack doesn't require much from its running backs, coach Jack Pardee would still like more than he gets from Lorenzo White (110 carries, 465 yards, 4 TDs). Leading rusher Allen Pinkett was dealt to New Orleans.

The only negative on the front five is age. But, led by All-Pros C Bruce Matthews and LG Mike Munchak, there's no sign of any slowdown. Tackles Don Maggs and David Williams and RG Doug Dawson are just fine, with John Flannery ready to step up.

The defensive front is just as good — and deep. Former All-Pro Lee Williams, plagued by nagging injuries, couldn't crack the lineup that featured ends William Fuller and Sean Jones and tackles Ray Childress, Jeff Alm, and Doug Smith. RLB Johnny Meads may be the weakest linebacker (and he isn't bad), with MLB Al Smith and LLB Lamar Lathon.

All-Pro LCB Cris Dishman keys a fine secondary. Darryl Lewis, Steve Jackson, and Plan B Jerry Gray will challenge nicked-up RCB Richard Johnson. Mike Dumas should battle FS Bo Orlando for a spot opposite SS Bubba McDowell.

AFC Central
CLEVELAND BROWNS
1991 Finish: Third
1992 Prediction: Second

Ed King

Bernie Kosar

Only a rash of injuries and limited depth kept rookie head coach Bill Belichick from turning the 3–13 Browns of 1990 into a play-off contender in '91. With another decent draft and fewer doctor visits, Cleveland could be on the way back in '92.

QB Bernie Kosar (307 for 494, 3,487 yards, 18 TDs) returns from what he — and the experts — call his best season. The 6–5, 215-pounder, written off by some, is still only 28. He's solid. But if Kosar goes down and Todd Philcox needs to take over, it could spell trouble.

Eric Metcalf, one of the most talented RBs in the league, has struggled. If Belichick gets him straightened out, the running game will improve. Leroy Hoard (37 car-ries, 154 yards, 2 TDs) bounced back from a so-so rookie year, and Kevin Mack (197 carries, 726 yards, 8 TDs) is fine. Top pick Tommy Vardell is strong and versatile.

Among the receivers, Webster Slaughter (64 catches, 906 yards, 3 TDs) is among the best, and Brian Brennan is reliable. But rangy Michael Jackson will have to turn it up a notch to replace Reggie Langhorne (gone via Plan B). A healthy Lawyer Tillman (out for two seasons) would certainly help. Tight end is an area of concern, though Plan B Pete Holohan joins Scott Galbraith.

LT Tony Jones and RG Ed King, the stickout rookie of '91, lead an improved offensive line. LG John Rienstra, C Mike Baab, and RT Dan Fike should return.

The defense, Belichick's specialty, was blown apart by injuries last year. Tackles Michael Dean Perry and James Jones could play for anyone; the ends can't. Draftee Bill Johnson helps.

The LBs were injury-riddled: two-time Pro Bowler Mike Johnson missed 11 games, and Plan Bs like David Brandon and Richard Brown won starting jobs. OLB Clay Matthews, at age 36, returns from a surprisingly fine season.

The secondary is in fair shape, with SS Eric Turner having shown Pro Bowl potential in his rookie year. Though Thane Gash left (Plan B), '91 injury victims Frank Minnifield and Ray Clayborn could be back, along with CB Randy Hilliard and S Vince Newsome.

AFC Central
PITTSBURGH STEELERS
1991 Finish: Second
1992 Prediction: Third

Louis Lipps   **Neil O'Donnell**

Here's a line that hasn't been written for 24 years: The Pittsburgh Steelers begin the new season with a new coach. After 23 campaigns (and four Super Bowl titles), Steeler coach Chuck Noll retired. The new man on the hot seat, Bill Cowher, should do better than Noll did in his first year (1–13), but that might not be good enough to satisfy the Pittsburgh boo-birds.

Cowher starts with a QB controversy: incumbent Bubby Brister (103 of 190, 1,350 yards, 9 TDs) vs. third-year man Neil O'Donnell (156 of 286, 1,963 yards, 11 TDs). Each started eight games in '91, and, despite a 2–6 record, O'Donnell was impressive. He might be the Steelers QB of the future.

Either way, the QB will have problems.

The running game is spotty. Merril Hoge (165 carries, 610 yards, 2 TDs) and Warren Williams (57 carries, 262 yards, 4 TDs) are ordinary. Tim Worley (22 carries, 117 yards, 0 TDs in only two games) was suspended by the NFL. But Barry Foster (96 carries, 488 yards, one TD) may be the best of the lot.

Top receiver Louis Lipps (55 catches, 671 yards, 2 TDs) is the club's top receiver, though he's lost at least a step. Things could get better if '91 high-round draft picks Jeff Graham and Ernie Mills show more than they did as rookies. Huge (6–5, 280) TE Eric Green (41 catches, 582 yards, 6 TDs before an ankle injury) is one of the NFL's best, and Adrian Cooper pairs well with Green.

The offensive line is a problem. C Dermontti Dawson is the standout; but RT Tunch Ilkin could give way to top draft Leon Searcy, and LT John Jackson and Gs Ariel Solomon and Carlton Haselrig are so-so.

NT Gerald Williams leads the defensive front. Ends Aaron Jones, Kenny Davidson, and Donald Evans haven't done it yet, especially against the pass. The linebacking is solid inside, with Hardy Nickerson, aging David Little, and draftee Levon Kirkland. Outside, Greg Lloyd is set, but Jerrol Williams may unseat Bryan Hinkle while the Steelers wait for Huey Richardson to develop.

The secondary quartet, featuring corners David Johnson and Rod Woodson and safeties Carnell Lake and Thomas Everett, is just fine. Depth is a question.

AFC Central
CINCINNATI BENGALS
1991 Finish: Fourth
1992 Prediction: Fourth

David Fulcher   **Boomer Esiason**

Hey, how bad a year could it have been in Cincinnati? The Bengals came from behind to beat the defending Super Bowl champion Giants. Trouble was, they won only two other games; they scored one TD or less in half of their games; and the defense ranked last in total defense, pass defense, and scoring defense. Outspoken coach Sam Wyche was canned, inexperienced David Shula was hired, and every day brought more bad news about the ball club.

So what's for '92? QB Boomer Esiason (233 of 413, 2,883 yards, 13 TDs, 16 interceptions) has had two straight off-years, and he's 31. Don Hollas probably can't do it. Top draft David Klingler might, if he's around.

With longtime Bengal star RB James

Brooks off to Cleveland (Plan B), Harold Green (158 carries, 731 yards, 2 TDs) and Craig Taylor are more important than ever. Any return by Ickey Woods to his old-time form would be deeply appreciated.

There's no reason to believe that WRs Eddie Brown (59 catches, 827 yards, 2 TDs), Tim McGee (51 catches, 802 yards, 4 TDs), draftee Carl Pickens, and TE Rodney Holman (31 catches, 445 yards, 2 TDs) can't become frightening offensive threats — provided Esiason gets the time to hit them.

That could be a problem. Age and injuries have taken a terrible toll on the front five, though T Anthony Munoz remains an awesome presence when healthy. Young Mike Arthur may have replaced C Bruce Kozerski, who had to fill in at guard and tackle in '91.

The defensive line, weak against the run, worse against the pass, counts on aging, banged-up NT Tim Krumrie as its leader. Alonzo Mitz and Natu Tuatagaloa finished up at the ends in '91. The Bengals will build their linebacker corps on outside men James Francis and '91 rookie Alfred Williams. There will be changes inside where Carl Zander left via Plan B.

Lewis Billups was another Plan B departure, leaving another hole in the secondary. RCB Eric Thomas has never fully recovered from knee surgery but should return, along with Wayne Haddix. David Fulcher, Barney Bussey, and first-rounder Darryl Williams are the safeties.

AFC West
KANSAS CITY CHIEFS
1991 Finish: Second
1992 Prediction: First

John Alt

Harvey Williams

The Kansas City Chiefs are close, maybe this close, to an AFC title. They're just a couple of players away. But one of those players is the quarterback, and the ability of ex-Seahawk Dave Kreig to run the show may be the key to the '92 season.

The Chiefs running game is super. In Christian Okoye, Barry Word, and Harvey Williams, they own the most powerful set of running backs in the conference. Between them, Okoye and Word had 1,715 yards and 13 rushing TDs last year, and Williams is a super talent. Blocking FB Bill Jones and third-down specialist Todd McNair are excellent.

But you need to throw the ball — and throw it down the field — to win in the NFL, and that could be a challenge. Kreig (185 of 285, 2,080 yards, 11 TDs for Seattle) was unprotected by the Seahawks. When Kaycee's Steve DeBerg (256 of 434, 2,965 yards, 17 TDs) took off for Tampa Bay, Kreig was the obvious choice. Backup Mark Vlasic is still around, but Kreig is the main man.

His new receivers lack an outside speed-burner, though Robb Thomas, Tim Barnett, Emile Harry, and J.J. Birden are more than adequate. There's a problem at TE, where Pete Holohan left via Plan B, and Jonathan Hayes has turned 30.

Similarly, the line manages to do the job without any superstars. The left side, tackle John Alt and guard Dave Szott, plus center Tim Grunhard are fine. But RG David Lutz is 33, and RT Derrick Graham makes too-frequent mistakes.

The defensive front seven is terrific. Ends Bill Smith and former All-Pro Bill Maas sandwich NT Dan Saleaumua. The LBs are even better. All-Pro ROLB Derrick Thomas may be the game's best; the rest, LOLB Chris Martin, backup Lonnie Marts, and ILBs Tracy Simien, Ervin Randle, and Dino Hackett, are tops.

The secondary is a major concern. Age and injuries are the factors. Former All-Pro Albert Lewis (knee) may be done; CB Kevin Ross is 30, FS Deron Cherry is 33. Jayice Pearson will get the call at LCB, with Kevin Porter the stickout at SS. Kaycee picked up Plan B CBs Ray Irwin and Tahaun Lewis and Ss Bennie Thompson, Martin Bayless, and top pick Dale Carter.

AFC West
LOS ANGELES RAIDERS
1991 Finish: Third
1992 Prediction: Second

Nick Bell

Howie Long

The Los Angeles Raiders' '92 season officially began in August with the induction of owner Al Davis into Pro Football's Hall of Fame. Will it end with Davis clutching the Super Bowl's Lombardi Trophy? Doubtful, unless the Raiders can solve their quarterback mess and find the Fountain of Youth for about half of their starters.

Lefty Todd Marinovich (23 of 40, 243 yards, 3 TDs) is probably the Raiders QB of the future, though his off-field behavior is a concern. But is it too early to give up on Jay Schroeder (189 of 356, 2,562 yards, 15 TDs)? The expensive Schroeder (he cost them All-Pro Jim Lachey) has all the tools, but have his coaches lost confidence in him?

With versatile RB Roger Craig gone to Minnesota (Plan B), the Raiders count on ex-

Colt superstar Eric Dickerson, Marcus Allen (63 carries, 287 yards, 2 TDs), and Nick Bell (78 carries, 307 yards, 3 TDs). All are solid; all are questionable. FB Steve Smith is a fine blocker.

L.A. picked up Plan Bs Mike Alexander from the Bills and Ron Brown from the Rams to bolster their corps of wide receivers. After a great 1990 season, Willie Gault (20 catches, 346 yards, 4 TDs) practically disappeared late last year. WRs Mervyn Fernandez (46, 694, one TD) and Tim Brown (36, 554, 5 TDs) are sound, and TE Ethan Horton (53, 650, 5 TDs) is excellent.

Up front on offense, age is a concern. G Max Montoya is 36, and C Don Mosebar is 30, so draftee T Greg Skrepenak is important. Tackles Bruce Wilkerson and Steve Wright are just adequate, but G Steve Wisniewski is among the best in the game.

The defensive line has a little trouble against the run. DEs Howie Long (age 32) and Greg Townsend and DTs Scott Davis and Bob Golic form a veteran quartet. Backup Nolan Harrison loves to rush the passer. Top pick, 340-pound Chester McGlockton, should help.

The linebacking group of Winston Moss, Riki Ellison, and Tom Benson is so-so. As long as Ronnie Lott stays healthy, the secondary will be fine. Plan B Dave Waymer arrives to back up Lott and FS Eddie Anderson. Terry McDaniel and Lionel Washington are experienced corners. The Raiders would like a little more speed here.

AFC West
DENVER BRONCOS
1991 Finish: First
1992 Prediction: Third

Mike Croel

John Elway

After coming off the deck (5–11 in 1990) to within four points of a Super Bowl trip in 1991, the Broncos enter '92 with a few questions, a bunch of answers, and another great shot at the top of the AFC.

QB John Elway (242 of 451, 3,253 yards, 13 TDs, 258 yards rushing) remains a major threat every time he runs onto the field. With Gary Kubiak retired, Denver needs a backup. Ninety-one draftee Shawn Moore may not be the answer, but '92 draftee Tommy Maddox might.

Bobby Humphrey's 1991 holdout paved the way for one-time Ram bust Gaston Green (261 carries, 1,037 yards, 4 TDs) to strut his stuff. There are still questions about his desire and durability. Steve Sewell (50 carries, 211 yards, 2 TDs) is an excellent blocker at FB. Humphrey went to Miami for RB Sammie Smith. Greg Lewis figures to be Green's backup.

The Broncos dealt Ricky Nattiel, reducing their WR depth. Michael Young (44 catches, 629 yards, 2 TDs, but difficult postseason disk surgery) and Derek Russell (21 catches, 317 yards, one TD) are the incumbents. There may be changes at TE, where vet Clarence Kay wasn't protected on Plan B.

The offensive line is a potential problem spot. LT Gerald Perry went to the Rams in the Green trade, creating a major hole. Harvey Salem should find a spot, perhaps at RT, leaving Jeff Davidson on the left, with Doug Widell and Sean Farrell at the guards and Keith Kartz at center. Age is a factor for Salem, Farrell, and RT Ken Lanier.

The defensive front (ends Warren Powers and Ron Holmes and NT Greg Kragen) is adequate — but that's all. The linebackers form the heart of the defense. Outside 'backers Simon Fletcher and Mike Croel, the Defensive Rookie of the Year, and inside men Karl Mecklenburg and Michael Brooks may be the AFC's best quartet.

Denver is in great shape at safety. FS Steve Atwater is among the game's best. SS Dennis Smith is an all-star, but CBs Tyrone Braxton and Wymon Henderson may be too small and a bit short on talent.

The Denver defense should remain as stingy as it was in '91; the offense needs to turn it up a notch or two.

AFC West
SAN DIEGO CHARGERS
1991 Finish: Fifth
1992 Prediction: Fourth

Junior Seau   **Rod Bernstine**

Fresh off a great coaching job, turning
Georgia Tech from a disaster area to a
football power, Bobby Ross takes over the
Chargers. It's disaster time again.

Ross inherits a ball club that sank from
6–10 in 1990 to 4–12 last year. The players
didn't like the coaches, the coaches didn't
like some players, and the rest is history.

Young John Friesz (262 of 487, 2,896 yards,
12 TDs) is the QB, for better or worse. The
Chargers were so confident of this one-time
U. of Idaho star that they traded former
starter Billy Joe Tolliver before opening day
last year.

The running game is solid. Powerful
Marion Butts (193 carries, 834 yards, 6 TDs)
is one of the NFL's best. Rod Bernstine,
given a shot when Butts held out during

summer '91, proved that he belongs, gaining 766 yards on 159 carries, a 4.8 average. Eric Bieniemy and Ronnie Harmon provide great depth. Blocker Craig McEwen is fine.

After his first minicamp, Ross announced his pleasure with his receiver group, especially if Shawn Jefferson keeps improving. If Anthony Miller is healthy and Nate Lewis reaches his potential, the Chargers will be OK here.

A return to health by Eric Moten and Harry Swayne on the left side of the Charger offensive front is vital. C Courtney Hall will be a great one, and RG David Richards is adequate. Broderick Thompson has been struggling at RT.

New defensive coordinator Bill Arnsparger looks to install a 4–3 look, which may move ROLB Leslie O'Neal to defensive end, opposite Burt Grossman and top draft Chris Mims. George Thornton and Joe Phillips would be the tackles. That would also move outstanding RILB Junior Seau to the outside, where he could terrorize enemy passers. Gary Plummer and Henry Rolling would join him.

The Chargers' weakest link is their secondary. Pro Bowler Gill Byrd, a natural safety and the league's leading interceptor over the past four years (27 interceptions; 6 in '91), is stuck at LCB because there is no one else. FS Stanley Richard has good potential, but there are huge holes elsewhere. Plan B safety Delton Hall will help if he recovers from off-season knee surgery.

AFC West
SEATTLE SEAHAWKS
1991 Finish: Fourth
1992 Prediction: Fifth

Cortez Kennedy

Eugene Robinson

Seattle Seahawks president Tom Flores, who led the Raiders to victories in Super Bowls XV and XVIII, adds the title of head coach in '92. But if he is to lead his new team to the big party, he'll have to find some new offensive magic. Seattle was 7–9 last year, and only the defense kept things from getting worse.

With Seattle's nine-year head coach Chuck Knox off for a return stay with the Rams, Flores immediately inherits a quarterback problem. Last year's No. 1 QB, Dave Kreig, is off to Kansas City via Plan B, leaving gigantic Dan McGwire (6-8, 245) and Kelly Stouffer to battle for the top job. If neither makes it, WLAF star Stan Gelbaugh may get the call.

Now in his seventh year, FB John L.

Williams (188 carries, 741 yards, 4 TDs, plus 61 catches for 499 yards receiving) is the leader of a weak group of Seattle runners. Backup FB James Jones (45 carries, 154 yards, 3 TDs) finished '91 as the starting RB.

The receivers have problems, too. Starting TE Mike Tice left for Minnesota (Plan B), creating a huge hole. (Travis McNeal should fill it.) Brian Blades (70 catches, 1,003 yards, 2 TDs) and Tommy Kane (50, 763, 2 TDs) are OK, but Doug Thomas or Dave Daniels must step up for more speed.

The line is about ⅗ complete. LT Andy Heck, RG Bryan Millard, and C Joe Tofflemire (if he's healthy) are set. LG Warren Wheat and RT Ronnie Lee are so-so, opening the way for top pick Ray Roberts.

The defense is Seattle's pride and joy. DRT Cortez Kennedy (72 tackles, 6½ sacks) has superstar potential. DLE Jacob Green is fine, though he was unsigned at camp time. DLT Jeff Bryant and DRE Tony Woods are solid, and ex-Viking Keith Millard could be great, if he's healthy.

Outside 'backers Terry Wooden and Rufus Porter (team-leading 10 sacks) have brilliant futures, but MLBs Dave Wyman and Darren Comeaux apparently can't get it done. Maybe draftee Bob Spitulski can.

The secondary is good now and should get even better. CBs Dwayne Harper and Patrick Hunter (sometimes inconsistent), SS Robert Blackmon, and FS Eugene Robinson will help Flores and defensive coordinator Tom Catlin sleep better.

You needn't be a genius to figure out what the Detroit Lions must do to win: Give the ball to super Barry Sanders.

National Football Conference Team Previews

NFC East
PHILADELPHIA EAGLES
1991 Finish: Third
1992 Prediction: First

Seth Joyner

Randall Cunningham

"If Randall comes back at full strength," says the Philadelphia Eagles' All-World defensive end Reggie White, "we'll win the Super Bowl." Pretty strong words from a very strong man. But if Randall Cunningham, who went down in the 1991 season opener, is ready to go and the Eagles generate some sort of running game, Philly in Pasadena is conceivable.

The Eagles own the game's best defense, led by the All-Pro defensive line, super OLB Seth Joyner, and hard-hitting S Andre Waters. Though DLE White got most of the notice up front, DLT Jerome Brown may have had a better season in '91. Add DRT Mike Pitts and outstanding DRE Clyde Simmons, and you have an incredible quartet. Swing tackle Mike Pitts is a fine backup, but ends Andy Harmon and Mike Flores need to improve for depth.

Joyner, *Sports Illustrated*'s choice as defensive player of the year, heads the linebacker corps from his spot on the left. William Thomas and Byron Evans complete the trio.

There's pressure on LCB Izel Jenkins, who replaced injured Pro Bowler Ben Smith. Smith may miss part of '92 as well. RCB Eric Allen is a Pro Bowler and Andre Waters and Wes Hopkins are fine safeties.

If Cunningham (30 TDs in '90) is ready, so are the Eagles. Four QBs tried to replace him in '91 with little success, save for well-traveled Jim McMahon (187 for 311, 2,239 yards, 12 TDs).

Any Eagle QB will be blessed with wonderful receivers, including Pro Bowl-quality Fred Barnett (62 catches, 948 yards, 4 TDs) and solid Calvin Williams (33 for 326, 3 TDs) on the outside. TE Keith Jackson (48 for 569, 5 TDs) is a frequent All-Pro, who isn't the world's best blocker.

James Joseph (135 carries, 440 yards, 3 TDs) was the rookie leader of a toothless Eagle running game last year. He's not the answer — but neither is Keith Byars (a better receiver). So top draftees Siran Stacey (Alabama) and Tony Brooks (Notre Dame) could be vital additions.

The offensive line? Young RT Antone Davis is coming; RG Ron Solt is gone; and folks like LT Ron Heller, LG Dennis McKnight, and C David Alexander need help.

NFC East
WASHINGTON REDSKINS
1991 Finish: First
1992 Prediction: Second

Ricky Ervins

Jeff Bostic

It started with a 1–3 preseason and lots of concern in Washington. It ended with 17 wins in 19 regular- and postseason contests and a smashing Super Bowl victory. The Redskins' 1991 season was straight out of a Hollywood movie. The big question now, of course, is: Will the sequel match the original?

As in Hollywood, the answer is: probably not. Repeating is difficult enough, and the 'Skins are beginning to show their age.

One thing is sure. When the season opens, QB Mark Rypien (249 of 421, 3,564 yards, 28 TDs) will be a wealthy young man. The 14th-highest-paid QB in the league last year will move up big time. With Cary Conklin and probably Jeff Rutledge on hand to back up, Stan Humphries will likely be elsewhere.

The emergence of Ricky Ervins (145 carries, 680 yards, 3 TDs) is a major plus, as Ernest Byner (274, 1,048, 5 TDs) and Gerald Riggs (78, 248) may have lost a step. The WRs are fabulous, led by the ever-dangerous "Posse" — Art Monk (71 catches, 1,049 yards, 8 TDs), Gary Clark (70, 1,340, 10 TDs), and Ricky Sanders (45, 580, 5 TDs). But Monk is 33, and Clark is 30, making ex-Michigan star Desmond Howard a vital addition. The 'Skins are plenty deep at TE.

The offensive line held opponents to a league-low nine sacks last year, led by All-Pro LT Jim Lachey. The rest of the current Hogs — RT Joe Jacoby, Gs Mark Schlereth and Raleigh McKenzie, and C Jeff Bostic — are terrific. Ed Simmons should be healthy, but Russ Grimm has retired.

There are questions on the defensive line where ends Charles Mann (knee) and Fred Stokes (shoulder) are returning from surgery. Ts Eric Williams and Tim Johnson are strong and quick. The LB crew is getting old. OLBs Andre Collins and Wilber Marshall led the team in tackles. MLB may be a problem.

At age 32, All-Pro CB Darrell Green remains football's fastest man. But for how long? CB Martin Mayhew and SS Danny Copeland are just ordinary. But FS Brad Edwards is first-rate.

The 'Skins will look to improve their punting game, but PK Chip Lohmiller is as good as they come.

NFC East
DALLAS COWBOYS
1991 Finish: Second
1992 Prediction: Third

Troy Aikman

Nate Newton

Did the Cowboys get too good too soon? Coach Jimmy Johnson's squad, which was 1–15 as recently as 1989, won their last five regular-season games in '91. That brought them from 6–5 to finish at 11–5. They won their first play-off game since '82 and their first on the road since '80.

Problem is, the Cowboys may not be that good. Sure, they won without No. 1 QB Troy Aikman (237 of 363, 2,754 yards, 11 TDs). Ex-Raider Steve Beuerlein (68 of 137, 909 yards, 5 TDs) filled in when a knee injury knocked Aikman out of the lineup.

RB Emmitt Smith, a Pro Bowler in each of his first two NFL years, led the league in rushing (1,563 yards on 365 carries, 12 TDs). He's terrific. But the rest of the Cowboys generated only 148 rushing yards, heaping more pressure on Smith.

WR Michael Irvin, now a certified All-Pro, led the league in receiving with 1,523 yards and 93 catches (with 8 TDs). No team in NFL history had produced both the rushing and receiving leaders in the same year. TE Jay Novacek (59 for 664 yards, 4 TDs) is first-rate. WR Alvin Harper (20 for 326) has superb potential, and Alexander Wright has speed to burn.

The Cowboys signed Plan B Frank Cornish in case their best lineman, C Mark Stepnoski, can't come to contract terms. Otherwise, Cornish tries at G, challenging Kevin Gogan and John Gesek. Huge RT Nate Newton joins LT Mark Tuinei and backup Erik Williams, who shows great promise.

DRT Russell Maryland started slowly but finished fast in '91, enhancing a young group (DLE Tony Tolbert, DLT Tony Casillas, and DRE Jim Jeffcoat). This group needs to put more pressure on enemy QBs.

Linebacking is a major worry. MLBs Jack Del Rio and Derrick Brownlow split via Plan B, inviting coach Johnson to try Vinson Smith or Ken Norton inside. MLB rookie Robert Jones and OLB Dixon Edwards should get a shot.

The secondary isn't much better. Only LCB Issiac Holt is among the league's best. RCB Larry Brown was a pleasant surprise in '91, joined by top pick Kevin Smith. Ray Horton and James Washington will be challenged at safety.

NFC East
NEW YORK GIANTS
1991 Finish: Fourth
1992 Prediction: Fourth

Rodney Hampton   **Leonard Marshall**

The mighty Super Bowl XXV champions turned mediocre long before Super Bowl XXVI. And unless coach Ray Handley manages to plug some huge gaps, the Giants will continue to sink — and he'll be unemployed. A 30–7 Monday night blow-out to hated Philadelphia and a 27–24 loss to 1-11 Cincinnati drove Giants fans nuts.

QB Jeff Hostetler (179 of 285, 2,032 yards, only 5 TDs) gets the call after recovering from a '91 back injury. He was the target of the boo-birds after the Giants got off slowly. Handley's conservative offense didn't help. Vet QB Phil Simms didn't find a new home, despite a full-time search last spring, so the backup spot remains his.

RB Rodney Hampton (256 carries, 1,059 yards, 10 TDs) blossomed big-time last year and may be joined by hefty Jarrod Bunch at FB. If ex-Cardinal Greg Amsler is on hand, longtime Giant Mo Carthon is gone.

The wideouts were OK, barely. Mark Ingram (51 catches, 824 yards, 3 TDs) and Stephen Baker (30 for 525, 4 TDs) will hold on. RB/kick-returner David Meggett (50 catches, 412 yards) is even more dangerous at the receiving end of a pass. But TE Howard Cross doesn't help the passing game, so the Giants spent their top draft pick on Notre Dame's Derek Brown.

The offensive line is the team's pride and joy. Ts Jumbo Elliott and Doug Riesenberg, Gs William Roberts and Eric Moore, and Pro Bowl C Bart Oates are excellent, and backups Brian Williams and Bob Kratch are first-rate.

If NT Erik Howard (back surgery) is healthy, the Giant defensive front is fine. DRE Leonard Marshall (11 sacks and plenty consistent) is a joy to watch and DLE Eric Dorsey is fine. Watch for Kanavis McGhee, a flop at LB, to get a shot at DE.

The once-feared NY linebackers aren't so scary anymore. ROLB Lawrence Taylor says '92 is his last year — maybe. Pepper Johnson is back inside, probably with free-agent Gary Reasons. Carl Banks is still first-rate at LOLB.

The secondary is slipping. LCB Mark Collins is fine, but RCB Everson Walls is through, and safeties Greg Jackson and Myron Guyton are mistake-prone. No. 2 draft pick Phillippi Sparks should help.

NFC East
PHOENIX CARDINALS
1991 Finish: Fifth
1992 Prediction: Fifth

Timm Rosenbach

Robert Massey

Phoenix coach Joe Bugel could well be the mystery guest on a new TV game show, *Where's My Line?* And if he and his staff don't find some fresh, quality bodies on both the offensive and defensive fronts, they could all wind up looking for jobs. The '91 Cards got off brilliantly, with road victories over the Rams and Eagles, then lost 12 of the last 14, wrecking the season.

A healthy QB Timm Rosenbach, who missed all of '91 (knee), would help, though he'll need up-front help. Chris Chandler (78 for 154, 846 yards, 5 TDs for Tampa Bay and Phoenix) will be ready if Rosenbach isn't. Top draft Tony Sacca will get a shot.

A Pro Bowl rookie in '90, RB Johnny Johnson slipped badly in '91 (196 carries, 666 yards, 4 TDs). Running mate Anthony

Thompson (126 carries, 376 yards, one TD) doesn't seem to own NFL speed.

If the QB gets time to pass, his wide receivers will catch the ball. Ernie Jones (61 catches, 957 yards, 4 TDs) and Ricky Proehl (55 catches, 766 yards, 2 TDs) are a capable pair. The addition of rookie Randal Hill (43 catches, 495 yards, one TD) added much needed speed. H-back Tim Jorden is barely adequate as a receiver, leaving the way for Plan B Butch Rolle to earn a start. TE Walter Reeves is basically a blocker.

The offensive line is, putting it mildly, awful. Trades and injuries have left the group toothless. Plan B T Mark May arrives from Washington, and new Card Danny Villa should help. But Tootie Robbins is gone, and Luis Sharpe may be, opening spots for Ed Cunningham and Jeff Christy.

The defense is a hair better than the offense. Pro Bowl SS Tim McDonald leads a secondary that also features young SS Michael Zordich, as well as CBs Aeneas Williams, hard-hitting Lorenzo Lynch, and, hopefully, a healthy CB Robert Massey.

The linebackers are OK. Leading-sacker Ken Harvey and Freddie Joe Nunn operate outside, with the Cards' top tackler Eric Hill on the inside, opposite folks like Garth Jax and Tyronne Stowe.

The line? Ugh. NG Eric Swann, who arrived without college experience, showed promise. DRE Mike Jones came fast at season's end. But ends Jeff Faulkner and Craig Patterson can't compete in the East.

NFC Central
CHICAGO BEARS
1991 Finish: Second
1992 Prediction: First

Mark Carrier   **Wendell Davis**

Coach Mike Ditka starts the '92 season with a new left hip and high expectations for his Chicago Bears. Chances are he'll limp less and worry more as the Bears try to bounce back from a late-season collapse that saw them lose four of their last six, including a 17–13 first-round play-off loss to Dallas.

"Offensively, I thought we had a decent year in '91," says Ditka. "Our running game bogged down because Neal Anderson [210 carries for 747 yards, 47 catches for 368 yards, nine TDs] and Brad Muster [90 for 412] missed a lot of time. We must produce more on first down and score more points."

The key is QB Jim Harbaugh (275 of 478, 3,121 yards, 15 TDs), perhaps Chicago's offensive MVP in '91. The self-confident

Harbaugh, stung by fans' criticism and the press in the past, sees a brilliant future. His backup is Peter Tom Willis.

The retirement of longtime All-Pro Jim Covert moves John Wojciechowski into the lineup at LT, with Keith Van Horne on the opposite side and Stan Thomas, who survived a bullet wound during a drive-by shooting last winter. Mark Bortz and Tom Thayer should return at the guards, with vet Jay Hilgenberg in the middle. The Bears signed Plan B long-snapper Mark Rodenhauser and drafted T Troy Auzenne early.

RBs Darren Lewis and Mark Green back up Muster and Anderson. Surprising Tom Waddle (55 catches for 599, 3 TDs), shockingly the Bears' new possession receiver, returns along with his partner Wendell Davis (61 for 945, 6 TDs). James Thornton returns at TE, where Cap Boso retired.

The Bears defense, except for a 52–14 pounding by the 49ers in the '92 regular-season finale, was fairly consistent. All-Pro MLB Mike Singletary is back for what he calls his last season. Vets John Roper and Jim Morrissey are the outside 'backers.

The line needs to pressure the QB, which means added responsibility for ends Richard Dent and Trace Armstrong and tackles Fridge Perry and Steve McMichael. Top pick Alonzo Spellman helps.

FS Mark Carrier (whose interceptions sank from 10 to two last year) keys the secondary (SS Shaun Gayle and corners Donnell Wooford and Lemuel Stinson).

NFC Central
DETROIT LIONS
1991 Finish: First
1992 Prediction: Second

Lomas Brown

Bennie Blades

The Lions come into the '92 season considerably changed from the group that opened the '91 campaign. Their coach, Wayne Fontes, once seen out the door, was the NFL's 1991 coach of the year. And the team, once the Central doormat, begins as defending NFC Central champion with its first play-off appearance since 1983.

As long as the league's premier RB Barry Sanders (342 carries for 1,548 yards, second in the NFL, and 16 TDs) stays healthy, the Lions should remain a Central power. Fontes hired a new offensive coordinator, veteran NFL head coach Dan Henning, in an attempt to get Sanders more involved in the passing game.

That will also depend on the Lions QB, either injury-prone Rodney Peete (116 of 194,

1,339 yards, 5 TDs before a season-ending Achilles injury) or '91 surprise Erik Kramer (136 of 265, 1,635 yards, 11 TDs).

The wide receivers — Willie Green (39 catches, 592 yards, 7 TDs), Mike Farr (42, 431, 1), Robert Clark (47, 640, 6), Brett Perriman (52, 668, 1), and Herman Moore (11, 135, 0) — should continue the major improvements that began last season.

The offensive line is a veteran group, led by tackles Lomas Brown and Eric Sanders, guards Eric Andolsek and Ken Dallafior (who took over when Mike Utley was paralyzed last season), and center Kevin Glover.

The healthy return of injured players is the major concern on defense. NT Jerry Ball, perhaps the NFL's best pass-rusher from that position, went down after a questionable block vs. the Jets. And OLB Mike Cofer might not make it back from season-ending knee surgery. That could leave Lawrence Pete in the middle, flanked by Dan Owens and Marc Spindler.

ILB Chris Spielman returns from his best NFL season to rejoin Dennis Gibson inside and Tracy Hayworth and George Jamison outside. The Lions tried to open their bank vaults — a positive sign — to pick up New Orleans free agent Pat Swilling, which shows that Fontes isn't totally satisfied with the LB corps.

The much-improved secondary features Pro Bowl FS Bennie Blades, along with hard-hitting cover men Ray Crockett and Melvin Jenkins and solid SS William White.

NFC Central
TAMPA BAY BUCCANEERS
1991 Finish: Fifth
1992 Prediction: Third

Lawrence Dawsey

Broderick Thomas

Coach Sam Wyche jumps from the Cincinnati frying pan into the Tampa Bay fire. (Don't those sound like great names for future franchises?) If Wyche, who tutored Boomer Esiason into stardom, can make Vinnie Testaverde (166 of 326, 1,994 yards, 8 TDs) into a successful pro quarterback, he'll own the town. If not, it's 38-year-old ex-Chief and ex-Buc Steve DeBerg, who probably can't win with this club, and another long season for Wyche — and Tampa Bay.

The Bucs went to Plan B to pick up some experience (Tampa Bay's roster was the NFL's youngest in '91) and plug some gaps. Ex-Bengal Bruce Reimers rejoins his old coach and should start at LG, which should help LT Paul Gruber. Tom McHale should compete for playing time. Center Tony

Mayberry should be back, along with RG Ian Beckles, RT Rob Taylor, and future star Charles McRae.

The receiving group is solid, led by WR Lawrence Dawsey (55 catches for 818 yards and 3 TDs), Mark Carrier (47 for 698, 2 TDs), and top rookie Courtney Hawkins. The TEs, like Ron Hall (31 for 284), should get more action under Wyche. The Bucs need an outside burner badly.

There's potential in the backfield where Reggie Cobb (196 carries for 752 yards, 7 TDs) is excellent. Robert Wilson is an excellent run-blocker, and Gary Anderson can still contribute.

One-time OLB Keith McCants, who shone at DE before shoulder surgery last season, may have to move back to linebacker to save his shoulder. Tough NT Tim Newton should return someplace in defensive coordinator Floyd Peters's schemes.

The linebacker group has potential, with RLB Broderick Thomas a future All-Pro. MLB Jesse Solomon makes the plays in the middle, with either Jimmy Williams or Kevin Murphy on the left side, depending upon McCants's status.

Free agent defensive backs Milton Mack (New Orleans), Joe King (Cleveland), and Sammy Lilly (Rams) will shake things up in the secondary, where only LCB Ricky Reynolds and SS Tony Covington seem assured of regaining their starting jobs.

The Bucs lost kicker Steve Christie to Buffalo via Plan B, a major shock.

NFC Central
MINNESOTA VIKINGS
1991 Finish: Third
1992 Prediction: Fourth

John Randle

Randall McDaniel

Veteran pro assistant and college head coach Dennis Green takes over a Minnesota Viking team that led the NFL in rushing for the first time ever. But it's likely to lose its leading ballcarrier, Herschel Walker (198 yards for 825 yards, 10 TDs), before the opening whistle.

Green got ex-Niner buddy Roger Craig as a Plan B from the Raiders. He'll replace Walker for a while. Terry Allen (120 carries for 563 yards, 2 TDs) is good, but sometimes inconsistent.

Rich Gannon (211 for 354, 2,166 yards, 12 TDs) is an adequate QB who must learn to throw the ball downfield more often. The receiving corps is solid, with Steve Jordan (57 catches for 638 yards and 2 TDs) among the NFL's best at TE and new backup help from ex-Seahawk Mike Tice. WR Cris Carter (72 for 962, 5 TDs) returns from his best year, and Anthony Carter (51 for 553, 5 TDs) remains a prime threat anywhere on the field.

The offensive line is the Vikings' finest unit. LG Randall McDaniel is the best of the group, with young Todd Kalis at the opposite guard, Gary Zimmerman and Tim Irwin at the tackles, and veteran Kirk Lowdermilk in the middle. Brian Habib and Craig Wolfley are the top backups, but more depth is needed here.

The Vikes made most of their off-season adjustments on defense. Ex-Giant Lorenzo Freeman and ex-Charger Skip McClendon arrive as Plan Bs up front. Pass-rusher supreme John Randle is back at DLE, with Chris Doleman on the other side. With Keith Millard gone at DRT, Ken Clarke, Henry Thomas, and top pick Robert Hams will battle for jobs.

Dallas's best tackler, LB Jack Del Rio, was a surprise Plan B addition. MLB Ray Berry wasn't the answer; RLB Mike Merriweather needed more help than he got from Jimmy Williams or injured Mark Dusbabek.

Ex-Saint FS Vencie Glenn and former Chief CB Anthony Parker join the battle for jobs in the secondary. Former All-Pro SS Joey Browner had an off-year in '91, as did RCB Reggie Rutland. Aging Felix Wright may have lost a step or two at FS. But LCB Carl Lee is first-rate, and nickel back Audray McMillan fills that task well.

NFC Central
GREEN BAY PACKERS
1991 Finish: Fourth
1992 Prediction: Fifth

Brian Noble

Tony Bennett

To its credit, Green Bay's ownership brought in a couple of winners to turn its 4–12 Pack around. Longtime Raider personnel expert Ron Wolf is the new general manager. Veteran 49er offensive expert Mike Holmgren is the new head coach. And the pair didn't waste a moment trying to put new faces into new places to rescue the franchise that hasn't won since Super Bowl II.

Holmgren, a master QB teacher with the Niners, will try to make ex-Falcon prospect Brett Favre the Packers QB of the future. But unless Don Majkowski (115 of 226, 1,362 yards, 3 TDs) makes a major comeback or Mike Tomczak (128 of 238, 1,490, 11) finally blossoms, the future may be now.

RB Keith Woodside is gone to Dallas,

and Darrell Thompson (141 for 471) is an average back; but Green Bay needs a new fullback — and soon. (Maybe it's Edgar Bennett.) Plan Bs Sanjay Beach and Kitrick Taylor join the WR corps, which lost Jeff Query and Erik Affholter. Sterling Sharpe (69 catches for 961 yards and 4 TDs) remains one of the NFL's best, with Ed West and Jackie Harris both solid at TE.

There will be changes up front where RT Tootie Robbins will allow Tony Mandarich to move to RG. A healthy Ken Ruettgers will help at LT. Rich Moran should return at LG, with James Campen solid at C.

There are even more adjustments on defense, particularly in the secondary. Ex-Giant Adrian White and ex-Colt Charles Washington will challenge holdover Mark Murphy. Ex-Bengal Lewis Billups moves in at one corner, with vets Jerry Holmes and LeRoy Butler battling top pick Terrell Buckley for the other spot. Vinnie Clark will remain at cornerback despite rumors that he would move to safety.

The defensive line is a major concern in Green Bay. Ends Robert Brown and Matt Brock surround noseman Esera Tuaolo. But the linebacker group is, perhaps, the Packers' best unit. ROLB Tony Bennett could be the top man, especially if he improves on pass coverage. Brian Noble is first-rate at LILB, with ROLB Scott Stephen and RILB Johnny Holland completing the quartet. There's good depth, too, mainly with Burnell Dent inside.

NFC West
ATLANTA FALCONS
1991 Finish: Second (tied)
1992 Prediction: First

Andre Rison   **Deion Sanders**

In *Inside Football '91*, we called the Falcons the NFC's team of the future. An 0–2 start shook us (and coach Jerry Glanville) a bit. But the Black Wave, motivated by Hammer's "2 Legit 2 Quit" rap video, won 8 of their last 11 and swept into the play-offs. The postseason victory at New Orleans was Atlanta's first play-off road win ever.

It should continue in '92, in the spanking new Georgia Dome, with just a couple of adjustments. QB Chris Miller (220 of 413, 3,103 yards, 26 TDs) is usually very good, but sometimes erratic. Backup Billy Joe Tolliver (40 of 82, 531 yards, 4 TDs) throws hard but often off-target.

Glanville must get Steve Broussard (99 carries, 449 yards, 4 TDs) back in gear to make the running game go. Eric Pegram

(101 for 349) and Tracy Johnson finished up after Broussard was injured last fall. First-rounder Tony Smith helps.

Atlanta has more WR depth than anyone in the NFL. Starters Andre Rison (81 catches, 976 yards, 12 TDs) and Michael Haynes (50 for 1,122, a spectacular 22.4 yards-per-catch average, and 11 TDs) are joined by ex-Oiler Plan B Drew Hill (90 catches, third in the league) and returnees Mike Pritchard, George Thomas, and other new additions.

Up front, 35-year-old LT Mike Kenn is among the NFL's best, but he *is* 35. Top pick Bob Whitfield fits right in. Chris Hinton is set at RT, with Houston Hoover (off major shoulder surgery) and Bill Fralic at the guards and Jamie Dukes in the middle. Without Reggie Redding, depth is needed.

Hotshot rookie Moe Gardner is back for his second year at NT. Ends Rick Bryan and Tim Green are OK, but a bigger pass-rush would help. ILB Jessie Tuggle leads the 'backers, but ILB John Rade and LLB Robert Lyles may both be on the down side. RLB Darion Conner is solid.

In the secondary, the corners are outstanding. RCB Deion Sanders, of Atlanta Braves fame, and LCB Tim McKyer, once a 49er superstar, each had six INTs in '91 to tie for the conference lead. Bruce Pickens may mature into a solid replacement. FS Scott Case and SS Brian Jordan are big hitters, though Jordan may opt to do his hitting for baseball's St. Louis Cardinals.

NFC West
SAN FRANCISCO 49ers
1991 Finish: Second (tied)
1992 Prediction: Second

John Taylor

Guy McIntyre

The team of the eighties, the four-time Super Bowl champion San Francisco 49ers, arrives at the crossroads in '92. In their heyday, everyone wanted to play for the Niners. But seven players left via Plan B last winter. So did several coaches.

San Fran may not be able to win without Joe Montana, but the superstar QB, who missed the entire '91 season, may not be ready for '92 — or ever. When premier backup QB Steve Young (180 for 279, 2,517 yards, 17 TDs, the NFL's top-rated passer) went down in November, Steve Bono (141 for 237, 1,617 yards, 11 scores) took over and was super. Trouble is, his mentor, Mike Holmgren, is now in Green Bay. It's a problem.

The "family" spirit left the club when Roger Craig and Ronnie Lott were allowed to leave before the '91 campaign. RBs Keith Henderson (137 carries, 561 yards) and tiny Dexter Carter (85 carries, 379 yards) tried to fill Craig's shoes with limited success. Highly rated Amp Lee should help.

Every team in the league would swap its receivers even up for San Francisco's. Despite a torn knee ligament, All-Pro Jerry Rice (80 catches, 1,206 yards, 14 TDs) was as good as ever in '91. John Taylor (64 for 1,011, 9 TDs) would be the main man anywhere else. If TE Brent Jones is healthy, the whole picture gets that much better.

Up front, depth is the only problem. RT Harris Barton is among the game's best. C Jesse Sapolu anchors the group that features T Steve Wallace and guards Guy McIntyre and Roy Foster, among others.

A season full of injuries wrecked the defensive line, where NT Michael Carter should again be joined by DEs Pierce Holt and Kevin Fagan. There are more problems if LOLB Charles Haley, a Pro Bowler after only six sacks in '91, gets his wish to be traded. If Haley goes, ex-Packer Tim Harris might be the No. 1 linebacker, though he might face a suspension for off-field behavior. ILB Mike Walter should be healthy again, joining Keith DeLong and Bill Romanowski. Injuries ruined the secondary last year, where a healthy SS Thane Gash could replace Plan B Dave Waymer. Corners Merton Hanks and Don Griffen return, along with FS Todd Bowles. Top draftee Dana Hall is an excellent choice.

NFC West
NEW ORLEANS SAINTS
1991 Finish: First
1992 Prediction: Third

Eric Martin   Bobby Hebert

From a 9–1 start in '91, the Saints lost two of their last six regular-season contests and their home play-off game against Atlanta to end with loads of doubt what should have been a glorious season.

It became apparent that Bobby Hebert (149 for 248, 1,676 yards, 9 TDs) is the Saints QB. Coach Jim Mora became ultra-cautious when backup Steve Walsh (141 of 255, 1,638 yards, 11 TDs) was in the lineup. Mike Buck could move up to No. 2 in '92.

Frequent injuries, Craig Heyward's weight, and other factors continue to wreck the Saints running game. Gill Fenerty and Buford Jordan finished last season, though backup halfback, rookie Fred McAfee, wound up as the team's top rusher (109 carries for 494 yards, 2 TDs). Top draft pick

Vaughn Dunbar could start soon.

The receivers are more than adequate, led by Eric Martin (66 catches for 803 yards, 4 TDs) and Floyd Turner (64 for 927, 8 TDs). Even with Quinn Early and Wesley Carroll on hand, there's not enough outside speed. TEs Hoby Brenner and John Tice are 33 and 32, respectively, a potential problem.

On the line, LG Jim Dombrowski is the team's best blocker. Chris Port and injury-returnees Steve Trapillo and Derek Kennard provide great guard depth. Aging Stan Brock may need some help at RT, with Richard Cooper on the left. Vet Joel Hilgenberg is solid at center.

The defensive front is first-rate, with Wayne Martin and Frank Warren surrounding NT Jim Wilks, who's now 34. There's no better linebacker quartet than All-Pros Sam Mills at LILB and $5.5-million man Pat Swilling at ROLB. There's no complaint with LOLB Rickey Jackson and RILB Vaughan Johnson. The Saints expect some help from OLB Joel Smeenge, but depth is a problem here.

There will be loads of changes in the New Orleans secondary, where newcomers Stan Petry, Jimmy Spencer, and third-rounder Tyrone Leggett will battle for playing time with FS Gene Atkins, CB Toi Cook, and SS Brett Maxie. That's vital because CB Vince Buck is coming back from a spinal injury. Lack of speed hurts this group.

Morten Andersen remains a superb kicker.

NFC West
LOS ANGELES RAMS
1991 Finish: Fourth
1992 Prediction: Fourth

Robert Delpino

Larry Kelm

Before the 1991 season, L.A. Rams head coach John Robinson cleaned out his defensive coaching staff. It was a last-ditch attempt to save a dying team. It failed. So, *after* the 1991 season, the Rams cleaned out Robinson and all of his coaches and brought one-time Ram coach Chuck Knox back from Seattle. It may be too little, too late.

The ball club's '91 highlight film could well have been called *The Silence of the Rams*. QB Jim Everett (277 for 490, 3,438 yards, only 11 TDs) has slipped badly the last couple of seasons. In Knox's last L.A. stay, he traded his No. 1 QB twice. Everett could be next.

Cleveland Gary (68 carries, 245 yards) could become the feature back in the new

Rams defense if he can stop putting the ball on the ground. Robert Delpino (10 TDs), with limited talent, is honest, hardworking, and effective both running and catching.

The receiving corps is good and could be better. Henry Ellard (64 catches, 1,052 yards, 3 TDs) and Flipper Anderson (32 for 530) form a fine starting pair. A healthy Arthur Cox is a must in three wide-receiver sets.

There will be changes up front. Duval Love split for Pittsburgh, and Bern Brostek and Tom Newberry will swap positions, with Brostek at center (backed up by veteran Blair Bush) and Newberry returning to guard where he won Pro Bowl honors. Robert Jenkins and aged Jackie Slater could be the tackles again.

A '91 rookie, DRE Robert Young, could be the anchor of a Ram front that needs to put more pressure on opposing passers. Unless he returns to LB full-time, vet Kevin Greene gets the call at DLE, with Alvin Wright and Mike Charles in the middle. Draftees Sean Gilbert and Marc Boutte will help.

The departures of corners Jerry Gray and Sammy Lilly via Plan B rob the Rams of their secondary depth. Still, the frontliners are young and improving. LCB Todd Lyght, who got his first rookie start at midseason last year, has super potential. FS Pat Terrell is an excellent cover man. RCB Darryl Henley and SS Michael Stewart are reasonable.

Look for Knox to clear out some more veterans as he tries to rebuild.

It's just about automatic. As long as Chicago's MLB Mike Singletary plays, we'll feature him on our All-Pro team.

1992
NFL
Draft List

The following abbreviations are used to identify the players' positions:

OFFENSE:
T = tackle; G = guard; C = center;
QB = quarterback; RB = running back;
WR = wide receiver; TE = tight end.

DEFENSE:
DE = defensive end; LB = linebacker;
DT = defensive tackle;
DL = defensive lineman;
DB = defensive back.

SPECIAL TEAMS:
P = punter; K = placekicker.

The number before each player's name indicates the overall position in which he was drafted.

Atlanta Falcons

8. Bob Whitfield, T, Stanford; 19. Tony Smith, RB, Southern Mississippi; 51. Chuck Smith, LB, Tennessee; 73. Howard Dinkins, LB, Florida St.; 104. Frankie Smith, DB, Baylor; 158. Terry Ray, DB, Oklahoma; 182. Tim Paulk, LB, Florida; 216. Derrick Moore, RB, Northeast Oklahoma; 217. Reggie Dwight, TE, Troy St.; 243. Keith Alex, T, Texas A&M; 270. Darryl Hardy, LB, Texas; 297. Robin Jones, DE, Baylor.

Buffalo Bills

27. John Fina, T, Arizona; 55. James Patton, DT, Texas; 83. Keith Goganious, LB, Penn St.; 111. Frank Kmet, DE, Purdue; 139. Matt Darby, DB, UCLA; 167. Nate Turner, TE, Nebraska; 195. Kurt Schulz, DB, Eastern Washington; 223. Leonard Humphries, DB, Penn St.; 251. Chris Walsh, WR, Stanford; 279. Barry Rose, WR, Wisconsin-Stevens Point; 307. Vince Marrow, TE, Toledo; 335. Matt Rodgers, QB, Iowa.

Chicago Bears

22. Alonzo Spellman, DE, Ohio St.; 49. Troy Auzenne, T, California; 80. Jeremy Lincoln, DB, Tennessee; 107. Will Furrer, QB, Virginia Tech; 134. Todd Harrison, TE, North Carolina St.; 161. Mark Berry, DB, Texas; 192. John Brown, WR, Houston; 246. Mirko Jurkovic, G, Notre Dame; 273. Nikki Fisher, RB, Virginia; 304. Louis Age, T, Southwestern Louisiana; 331. Chris Wilson, LB, Oklahoma.

Cincinnati Bengals

6. David Klingler, QB, Houston; 28. Darryl Williams, DB, Miami (FL); 31. Carl Pickens, WR, Tennessee; 84. Leonard Wheeler, DB, Troy St.; 88. Ricardo McDonald, LB, Pittsburgh; 115. Craig Thompson, TE, North Carolina A&T; 142. Chris Burns, DT, Middle Tennessee St.; 172. Lance Olberding, T, Iowa; 199. Roosevelt Nix, DE, Central St. (Ohio); 226. Ostell Miles, RB, Houston; 256. Horace Smith, DB, Oregon Tech; 283. John Earle, T, Western Illinois; 310. Eric Shaw, LB, Louisiana Tech.

Cleveland Browns

9. Tommy Vardell, RB, Stanford; 52. Patrick Rowe, WR, San Diego St.; 65. Bill Johnson, DT, Michigan St.; 78. Gerald Dixon, LB, South Carolina; 143. Rico Smith, WR, Colorado; 163. George Williams, DT, Notre Dame; 177. Selwin Jones, DB, Colorado St.; 233. Tim Hill, DB, Kansas; 260. Marcus Lowe, DT, Baylor; 289. Augustin Olobla, WR, Washington St.; 316. Keithen McCant, QB, Nebraska; 329. Tim Simpson, C-G, Illinois.

Dallas Cowboys

17. Kevin Smith, DB, Texas A&M; 24. Robert Jones, LB, East Carolina; 36. Jimmy Smith, WR, Jackson St.; 37. Darren Woodson, DB, Arizona St.; 58. Clayton Holmes, DB, Carson-Newman; 82. James Brown, T, Virginia St.; 109. Tom Myslinski, G-C, Tennessee; 120. Greg Bruggs, DB, Texas Southern; 121. Roderick Milstead, G, Delaware St.; 149. Fallon Wacasey, TE, Tulsa; 248. Nate Kirtman, DB, Pomona-Pitzer; 250. Chris Hall, DB, East Carolina; 275. John Terry, G, Livingstone; 302. Tim Daniel, WR, Florida A&M; 317. Don Harris, DB, Texas Tech.

Denver Broncos

25. Tommy Maddox, QB, UCLA; 54. Shane Dronett, DE, Texas; 110. Chuck Johnson, G, Texas; 137. Frank Robinson, DB, Boise St.; 170. Ron Geater, DE, Iowa; 181. Jim Johnson, T, Michigan St.; 193. Jon Bostick, WR, Nebraska; 208. Dietrich Lockridge, G, Jackson St.; 249. Muhammad Oliver, DB, Oregon; 278. Bob Meeks, C, Auburn; 305. Cedric Tillman, WR, Alcorn St.; 334. John Granby, DB, Virginia Tech.

Detroit Lions

26. Robert Porcher, DT, South Carolina St.; 53. Tracy Scroggins, LB, Tulsa; 56. Jason Hanson, K, Washington St.; 81. Thomas McLemore, TE, Southern; 145. Larry Tharpe, T, Tennessee St.; 221. Willie Clay, DB, Georgia Tech; 306. Ed Tillison, RB, Northwest Missouri St.

Green Bay Packers

5. Terrell Buckley, DB, Florida St.; 34. Mark D'Onofrio, LB, Penn St.; 62. Robert Brooks, WR, South Carolina; 103. Edgar Bennett, RB, Florida St.; 119. Dexter McNabb, RB, Florida; 130. Orlando McCay, WR, Washington; 157. Mark Chmura, TE, Boston College; 190. Christopher Holder, WR, Tuskegee; 230. Ty Detmer, QB, Brigham Young; 240. Shazzon Bradley, DT, Tennessee; 257. Andrew Oberg, T, North Carolina; 287. Gabriel Mokwuah, LB, American International; 314. Brett Collins, LB, Washington.

Houston Oilers

50. Eddie Robinson, LB, Alabama St.; 77. Corey Harris, RB, Vanderbilt; 108. Mike Mooney, T, Georgia Tech; 133. Joe Bowden, LB, Oklahoma; 135. Tony Brown, DB, Fresno St.; 136. Tim Roberts, DT, Southern Mississippi; 162. Mario Bailey, WR, Washington; 189. Elbert Turner, WR, Illinois; 220. Bucky Richardson, QB, Texas A&M; 247. Bernard Dafney, T, Tennessee; 274. Dion Johnson, WR, East Carolina; 301. Anthony Davis, LB, Utah; 332. Joe Wood, K, Air Force.

Indianapolis Colts

1. Steve Entman, DT, Washington; 2. Quentin Coryatt, LB, Texas A&M; 29. Ashley Ambrose, DB, Mississippi Valley St.; 85. Rodney Culver, RB, Notre Dame; 105. Anthony McCoy, DL, Florida; 113. Maury Toy, RB, UCLA; 141. Shoun Habersham, WR, Tennessee-Chattanooga; 169. Derek Steele, DE, Maryland; 197. Jason Belser, DB, Oklahoma; 212. Ronald Humphrey, RB, Mississippi Valley St.; 225. Eddie Miller, WR, South Carolina; 253. Steven Grant, LB, West Virginia; 309. Michael Brandon, DE, Florida.

Kansas City Chiefs

20. Dale Carter, DB, Tennessee; 40. Matt Blundin, QB, Virginia; 101. Mike Evans, DL, Michigan; 159. Tony Smith, WR, Notre Dame; 186. Erick Anderson, LB, Michigan; 213. Jim Jennings, G, San Diego St.; 244. Jay Leeuwenburg, C, Colorado; 271. Gerry Ostroski, G, Tulsa; 298. Doug Rigby, DE, Wyoming; 325. Corey Williams, DB, Oklahoma St.

Los Angeles Raiders

16. Chester McGlockton, DT, Clemson; 32. Greg Skrepenak, T, Michigan; 128. Derrick Hoskins, DB, Southern Mississippi; 156. Tony Rowell, C, Florida; 185. Kevin Smith, RB, UCLA; 268. Alberto White, LB, Texas Southern; 324, Tom Roth, G, Southern Illinois.

Los Angeles Rams

3. Sean Gilbert, DT, Pittsburgh; 30. Steve Israel, DB, Pittsburgh; 57. Mark Boutte, DT, Louisiana State; 60. Todd Kinchen, WR, Louisiana State; 87. Shawn Harper, T, Indiana; 114. Chris Crooms, DB, Texas A&M; 144. Joe Campbell, RB, Middle Tennessee St.; 171. Darryl Ashmore, T, Northwestern; 173. Curtis Cotton, DB, Nebraska; 198. Ricky Jones, QB, Alabama St.; 228. T.J. Rubley, QB, Tulsa; 255. Tim Lester, RB, Eastern Kentucky; 281. Brian Townsend, LB, Michigan; 282. Brian Thomas, WR, Southern; 312. Kelvin Harris, C, Miami.

Miami Dolphins

7. Troy Vincent, DB, Wisconsin; 12. Marco Coleman, LB, Georgia Tech; 43. Eddie Blake, G, Auburn; 70. Larry Webster, DT, Maryland; 97. Dwight Holler, LB, North Carolina; 124. Christopher Perez, T, Kansas; 155. Roosevelt Collins, LB, TCU; 191. Dave Moore, TE, Pittsburgh; 209. Andre Powell, LB, Penn St.; 236. Tonhy Tellington, DB, Youngstown St.; 267. Raoul Spears, RB, USC; 294. Lee Miles, WR, Baylor; 296. Mark Barsotti, QB, Fresno St.; 321. Milton Biggins, TE, Western Kentucky; 328. Kameno Bell, RB, Illinois.

Minnesota Vikings

39. Robert Harris, DE, Southern; 98. Roy Barker, DT, North Carolina; 125. Ed McDaniel, LB, Clemson; 152. Mike Gaddis, RB, Oklahoma; 183. David Wilson, DB, California; 210. Luke Fisher, TE, East Carolina; 227. Brad Johnson, QB, Florida St.; 237. Ronnie West, WR, Pittsburgh; 264. Brad Culpepper, DT, Florida; 295. Charles Evans, RB, Clark-Atlanta; 322. Joe Randolph, WR, Elon.

New England Patriots

13. Eugene Chung, T, Virginia Tech; 35. Rodney Smith, DB, Notre Dame; 64. Todd Collins, LB, Carson-Newman; 71. Kevin Turner, RB, Alabama; 90. Dion Lambert, DB, UCLA; 93. Darren Anderson, DB, Toledo; 116. Dwayne Sabb, LB, New Hampshire; 165. Tracy Boyd, G, Elizabeth City St.; 176. Wayne Hawkins, WR,

Southwest Minnesota; 194. Jim Gray, DT, West Virginia; 204. Scott Lockwood, RB, USC; 205. Sam Gash, RB, Penn St.; 232. David Dixon, DT, Arizona St.; 261. Turner Baur, TE, Stanford; 277. Steve Gordon, C, California; 288. Mike Petko, LB, Nebraska; 333. Freeman Baysinger, WR, Humboldt St.

New Orleans Saints
21. Vaughn Dunbar, RB, Indiana; 72. Tyrone Legette, DB, Nebraska; 95. Gene McGuire, C, Notre Dame; 106. Sean Lumpkin, DB, Minnesota; 138. Torrance Small, WR, Alcorn St.; 164. Kary Vincent, DB, Texas A&M; 218. Robert Stewart, DT, Alabama; 245. Donald Jones, LB, Washington; 276. Marcus Dowdell, WR, Tennessee St.; 303. Mike Gisler, G, Houston; 330. Scott Adell, T, North Carolina St.

New York Giants
14. Derek Brown, TE, Notre Dame; 41. Phillippi Sparks, CB, Arizona St.; 69. Aaron Pierce, TE, Washington; 99. Keith Hamilton, DE, Pittsburgh; 126. Michael Wright, DB, Washington; 153. Stacey Dillard, DT, Oklahoma; 180. Corey Widmer, DT, Montana St.; 211. Kent Graham, QB, Ohio St.; 238. Anthony Prior, DB, Washington St.; 265. George Rooks, DT, Syracuse; 292. Nate Singleton, WR, Grambling; 323. Charles Swann, WR, Indiana St.

New York Jets
15. Johnny Mitchell, TE, Nebraska; 42. Kurt Barber, LB, USC; 68. Siupeli Malamala, T, Washington; 96. Keo Coleman, LB, Mississippi St.; 127. Cal Dixon, C, Florida; 154. Glen Cadrez, LB, Houston; 166. Jeff Blake, QB, East Carolina; 219. Vincent Brownlee, WR, Mississippi; 266. Mario Johnson, DT-G, Missouri; 293. Eric Boles, WR, Central Washington.

Philadelphia Eagles
48. Siran Stacey, RB, Alabama; 75. Tommy Jeter, DT, Texas; 92. Tony Brooks, RB, Notre Dame; 102. Casey Weldon, QB, Florida St.; 129. Corey Barlow, DB, Auburn; 160. Jeff Snyder, WR, Hawaii; 187. William

Boatwright, G, Virginia Tech; 214. Charles Bullough, LB, Michigan St.; 241. Ephesians Bartley, LB, Florida; 272. Mark McMillan, DB, Alabama; 299. Pumpy Todors, P, Tennessee-Chattanooga; 326. Brandon Houston, T, Oklahoma.

Phoenix Cardinals
46. Tony Sacca, QB, Penn St.; 61. Ed Cunningham, C, Washington; 91. Jeff Christy, T, Pittsburgh; 100. Michael Bankston, DT, Sam Houston St.; 146. Brian Brauninger, T, Oklahoma; 175. Derek Ware, TE, Central St. (OK); 202. Eric Blount, WR, North Carolina; 229. David Henson, DT, Arkansas Central; 239. Tyrone Williams, WR, Western Ontario; 259. Reggie Yarbrough, RB, Cal State-Fullerton; 286. Robert Baxley, T, Iowa; 313. Lance Wilson, DT, Texas.

Pittsburgh Steelers
11. Leon Searcy, T, Miami (FL); 38. Levon Kirkland, LB, Clemson; 91. Joel Steed, DT, Colorado; 94. Charles Davenport, WR, North Carolina St.; 123. Alan Haller, DB, Michigan St.; 179. Russ Campbell, TE, Kansas St.; 188. Scottie Graham, RB, Ohio St.; 203. Darren Perry, DB, Penn St.; 206. Hesham Ismail, G, Florida; 215. Nate Williams, DT, Mississippi St.; 235. Elnardo Webster, LB, Rutgers; 262. Mike Saunders, RB, Iowa; 291. Kendall Gammons, G, Pittsburgh St.; 318. Cornelius Benton, QB, Connecticut.

San Diego Chargers
23. Chris Mims, DE, Tennessee; 33. Marquez Pope, DB, Fresno St.; 63. Ray Ethridge, WR, Pasadena City; 117. Curtis Whitley, C, Clemson; 131. Kevin Little, LB, North Carolina A&T; 140. Eric Jonassen, T, Bloomsburg St.; 147. Reggie White, DT, North Carolina A&T; 174. Deems May, TE, North Carolina; 201. James Fuller, DB, Portland St.; 231. Johnnie Barnes, WR, Hampton; 258. Arthur Paul, DT, Arizona St.; 285. Keith McAfee, RB, Texas A&M; 315. Carlos Huerta, K, Miami (FL).

San Francisco 49ers

18. Dana Hall, DB, Washington; 45. Amp Lee, RB, Florida St.; 76. Brian Bollinger, G, North Carolina; 89. Mark Thomas, DE, North Carolina St.; 150. Damien Russell, DB, Virginia Tech; 242. Darien Hagen, QB, Colorado; 269. Corey Mayfield, DE, Oklahoma; 300. Tom Covington, TE, Georgia Tech; 327. Matt La Bounty, DE, Oregon.

Seattle Seahawks

10. Ray Roberts, T, Virginia; 66. Bobby Spitulski, LB, Central Florida; 122. Gary Dandridge, DB, Appalachian St.; 151. Michael Bates, WR, Arizona; 178. Mike Frier, DT, Appalachian St.; 207. Muhammad Shamsid-Deen, RB, Tennessee-Chattanooga; 234. Larry Stayner, TE, Boise St.; 263. Anthony Hamlet, DE, Miami (FL); 290. Kris Rongen, G, Washington; 319. Chico Fraley, LB, Washington; 320. John MacNeill, DE, Michigan St.

Tampa Bay Buccaneers

44. Courtney Hawkins, WR, Michigan St.; 59. Mark Wheeler, DT, Texas A&M; 79. Tyji Armstrong, TE, Mississippi; 86. Craig Erickson, QB, Miami (FL); 118. Rogerick Green, DB, Kansas St.; 132. Santana Dotson, DE, Baylor; 148. James Malone, LB, UCLA; 184. Ken Swilling, DB, Georgia Tech; 200. Anthony McDowell, RB, Texas Tech; 222. Mike Pawlawski, QB, California; 254. Elijah Alexander, LB, Kansas St.; 284. Mazio Royster, RB, USC; 311. Klaus Wilmsmeyer, P, Louisville.

Washington Redskins

4. Desmond Howard, WR, Michigan; 47. Shane Collins, DT, Arizona St.; 74. Paul Siever, G, Penn St.; 112. Chris Hakel, QB, William & Mary; 168. Ray Rowe, TE, San Diego St.; 196. Calvin Holmes, DB, USC; 224. Darryl Moore, G, Texas-El Paso; 252. Boone Powell, LB, Texas; 280. Tony Barker, LB, Rice; 308. Terry Smith, WR, Penn St.; 226. Matt Elliott, C, Michigan.

1991 Statistics

Leading Rushers	Att.	Yards	Avg.	TDs
AFC				
Thomas, Buff.	288	1407	4.9	7
Green, Den.	261	1037	4.0	4
Okoye, K.C.	225	1031	4.6	9
Russell, N.E.	266	959	3.6	4
Higgs, Mia.	231	905	3.9	4
Butts, S.D.	193	834	4.3	6
Bernstine, S.D.	159	766	4.8	8
Williams, Sea.	188	741	3.9	4
Green, Cin.	158	731	4.6	2
Thomas, Jets	189	728	3.9	3
Mack, Clev.	197	726	3.7	8
Pinkett, Hou.	171	720	4.2	9
Word, K.C.	160	684	4.3	4
Baxter, Jets	184	666	3.6	11
K. Davis, Buff.	129	624	4.8	4
Hoge, Pitt.	165	610	3.7	2
Craig, Raiders	162	590	3.6	1
Brooks, Cin.	152	571	3.8	2
Harmon, S.D.	89	544	6.1	1
Dickerson, Ind.	167	536	3.2	2

Leading Rushers	Att.	Yards	Avg.	TDs
NFC				
E. Smith, Dall.	365	1563	4.3	12
B. Sanders, Det.	342	1548	4.5	16
Hampton, Giants	256	1059	4.1	10
Byner, Wash.	274	1048	3.8	5
Walker, Minn.	198	825	4.2	10
Cobb, T.B.	196	752	3.6	7
Anderson, Chi.	210	747	3.6	6
Delpino, Rams	214	688	3.2	9
Ervins, Wash.	145	680	4.7	3
Johnson, Phoe.	196	666	3.4	4
Allen, Minn.	120	563	4.7	2
Henderson, S.F.	137	561	4.1	2
McAfee, N.O.	109	494	4.5	2
Fenerty, N.O.	139	477	3.4	3
Thompson, G.B.	141	471	3.3	1
Broussard, Atl.	99	449	4.5	4
Joseph, Phil.	135	440	3.3	3

Leading Passers	Att.	Comp.	Yds. Gnd.	TD Pass	Int.	Rating
AFC						
Kelly, Buff.	474	304	3844	33	17	97.6
Kosar, Clev.	494	307	3487	18	9	87.8
Marino, Mia.	549	318	3970	25	13	85.8
Krieg, Sea.	285	187	2080	11	12	82.5
Moon, Hou.	655	404	4690	23	21	81.7
DeBerg, K.C.	434	256	2965	17	14	79.3
O'Donnell, Pitt.	286	156	1963	11	7	78.8
O'Brien, Jets	489	287	3300	10	11	76.6
Elway, Den.	451	242	3253	13	12	75.4
George, Ind.	485	292	2910	10	12	73.8
Esiason, Cin.	413	233	2883	13	16	72.5
Millen, N.E.	409	246	3073	9	18	72.5
Schroeder, Raiders	357	189	2562	15	16	71.4
Friesz, S.D.	487	262	2896	12	15	67.1

Leading Passers	Att.	Comp.	Yds. Gnd.	TD Pass	Int.	Rating
NFC						
Young, S.F.	279	180	2517	17	8	101.8
Rypien, Wash.	421	249	3564	28	11	97.9
Bono, S.F.	237	141	1617	11	4	88.5
Aikman, Dall.	363	237	2754	11	10	86.7
Hostetler, Giants	285	179	2032	5	4	84.1
Gannon, Minn.	354	211	2166	12	6	81.5
Miller, Atl.	413	220	3103	26	18	80.6
McMahon, Phil.	311	187	2239	12	11	80.3
Walsh, N.O.	255	141	1638	11	6	79.5
Hebert, N.O.	248	149	1676	9	8	79.0
Harbaugh, Chi.	478	275	3121	15	16	73.7
Tomczak, G.B.	238	128	1490	11	9	72.6
Kramer, Det.	265	136	1635	11	8	71.8
Everett, Rams	490	277	3438	11	20	68.9

Leading Receivers	No.	Yards	Avg.	TDs
AFC				
Jeffires, Hou.	100	1181	11.8	7
Hill, Hou.	90	1109	12.3	4
Cook, N.E.	82	808	9.9	3
Reed, Buff.	81	1113	13.7	10
Toon, Jets	74	963	13.0	0
Brooks, Ind.	72	888	12.3	4
Duper, Mia.	70	1085	15.5	5
Clayton, Mia.	70	1053	15.0	12
Blades, Sea.	70	1003	14.3	2
Givins, Hou.	70	996	14.2	5
Moore, Jets	70	987	14.1	5
Fryar, N.E.	68	1014	14.9	3
Slaughter, Clev.	64	906	14.2	3
Thomas, Buff. (RB)	62	631	10.2	5
Williams, Sea. (RB)	61	499	8.2	1
Hester, Ind.	60	753	12.6	5
Brown, Cin.	59	827	14.0	2

Leading Receivers	No.	Yards	Avg.	TDs
NFC				
Irvin, Dall.	93	1523	16.4	8
Rison, Atl.	81	976	12.0	12
Rice, S.F.	80	1206	15.1	14
C. Carter, Minn.	72	962	13.4	5
Monk, Wash.	71	1049	14.8	8
Clark, Wash.	70	1340	19.1	10
Sharpe, G.B.	69	961	13.9	4
E. Martin, N.O.	66	803	12.2	4
Ellard, Rams	64	1052	16.4	3
Taylor, S.F.	64	1011	15.8	9
Turner, N.O.	64	927	14.5	8
Barnett, Phil.	62	948	15.3	4
Byars, Phil. (RB)	62	564	9.1	3
E. Jones, Phoe.	61	957	15.7	4
Davis, Chi.	61	945	15.5	6
Novacek, Dall.	59	664	11.3	4
Jordan, Minn.	57	638	11.2	2

Leading Interceptors	No.	Yards	Long	TDs
AFC				
Lott, Raiders	8	52	27	0
Dishman, Hou.	6	61	43	0
Byrd, S.D.	6	48	22	0
Odomes, Buff.	5	120	48	1
Atwater, Den.	5	104	49	0
Oliver, Mia.	5	80	37	0
D. Smith, Den.	5	60	39	0
NFC				
Crockett, Det.	6	141	96	1
Sanders, Atl.	6	119	55	1
A. Williams, Phoe.	6	60	32	0
McKyer, Atl.	6	24	24	0
Atkins, N.O.	5	198	79	0
Browner, Minn.	5	97	45	0
Marshall, Wash.	5	75	54	1

Leading Scorers, Kicking	XP	XPA	FG	FGA	Pts.
AFC					
Stoyanovich, Mia.	28	29	31	37	121
Jaeger, Raiders	29	30	29	34	116
Treadwell, Den.	31	32	27	36	112
Lowery, K.C.	35	35	25	30	110
Norwood, Buff.	56	58	18	29	110
Leahy, Jets	30	30	26	37	108
Kasay, Sea.	27	28	25	31	102
Anderson, Pitt.	31	31	23	33	100
Breech, Cin.	27	27	23	29	96
Carney, S.D.	31	31	19	29	88
NFC					
Lohmiller, Wash.	56	56	31	43	149
Willis, Dall.	37	37	27	39	118
Andersen, N.O.	38	38	25	32	113
Ruzek, Phil.	27	29	28	33	111
Murray, Det.	40	40	19	28	97
N. Johnson, Atl.	38	39	19	23	95
Cofer, S.F.	49	50	14	28	91
Bahr, Giants	24	25	22	29	90
Butler, Chi.	32	34	19	29	89
Jacke, G.B.	31	31	18	24	85
Reveiz, Minn.	34	35	17	24	85

Leading Scorers, Touchdowns	TDs	Rush	Rec.	Ret.	Pts.
AFC					
Clayton, Mia.	12	0	12	0	72
Thomas, Buff.	12	7	5	0	72
Baxter, Jets	11	11	0	0	66
Hoard, Clev.	11	2	9	0	66
Mack, Clev.	10	8	2	0	60
Pinkett, Hou.	10	9	1	0	60
Reed, Buff.	10	0	10	0	60
Okoye, K.C.	9	9	0	0	54
Bernstine, S.D.	8	8	0	0	48
Lofton, Buff.	8	0	8	0	48

Leading Scorers, Touchdowns	TDs	Rush	Rec.	Ret.	Pts.
NFC					
B. Sanders, Det.	17	16	1	0	102
Rice, S.F.	14	0	14	0	84
E. Smith, Dall.	13	12	1	0	78
Rison, Atl.	12	0	12	0	72
Haynes, Atl.	11	0	11	0	66
Riggs, Wash.	11	11	0	0	66
Workman, G.B.	11	7	4	0	66
Clark, Wash.	10	0	10	0	60
Delpino, Rams	10	9	1	0	60
Hampton, Giants	10	10	0	0	60
Walker, Minn.	10	10	0	0	60

Leading Punters	No.	Yards	Long	Avg.
AFC				
Roby, Mia.	54	2466	64	45.7
Gossett, Raiders	67	2961	61	44.2
Gr. Montgomery, Hou.	48	2105	60	43.9
Johnson, Cin.	64	2795	62	43.7
Tuten, Sea.	49	2106	60	43.0
Stark, Ind.	82	3492	65	42.6
Hansen, Clev.	80	3397	65	42.5
Horan, Den.	72	3012	71	41.8
Stryzinski, Pitt.	74	2996	63	40.5
Barker, K.C.	57	2303	57	40.4
Kidd, S.D.	76	3064	60	40.3
McCarthy, N.E.	66	2650	93	40.2
Aguiar, Jets	64	2521	61	39.4
Mohr, Buff.	54	2085	58	38.6

Leading Punters	No.	Yards	Long	Avg.
NFC				
Newsome, Minn.	68	3095	65	45.5
Camarillo, Phoe.	76	3445	60	45.3
Barnhardt, N.O.	86	3743	61	43.5
Landeta, Giants	64	2768	61	43.3
Fulhage, Atl.	81	3470	60	42.8
Saxon, Dall.	57	2426	64	42.6
Feagles, Phil.	87	3640	77	41.8
Arnold, Det.	75	3092	63	41.2
Buford, Chi.	69	2814	64	40.8
McJulien, G.B.	86	3473	62	40.4
Royals, T.B.	84	3389	56	40.3
Goodburn, Wash.	52	2070	61	39.8
Prokop, S.F.	40	1541	58	38.5
Hatcher, Rams	63	2403	52	38.1

Leading Punt Returners	No.	Yards	Avg.	TDs
AFC				
Woodson, Pitt.	28	320	11.4	0
Brown, Raiders	29	330	11.4	1
Taylor, S.D.	28	269	9.6	0
Warren, Sea.	32	298	9.3	1
Miller, Mia.	28	248	8.9	0
Henderson, N.E.	27	201	7.4	0
V. Johnson, Den.	24	174	7.3	0
Mathis, Jets	23	157	6.8	0
NFC				
Gray, Det.	25	385	15.4	1
Mitchell, Wash.	45	600	13.3	2
Martin, Dall.	21	244	11.6	1
Meggett, Giants	28	287	10.3	1
Drewrey, T.B.	38	360	9.5	0
Sikahema, G.B.	26	239	9.2	0
Turner, Rams	23	201	8.7	0
Taylor, S.F.	31	267	8.6	0
V. Buck, N.O.	31	260	8.4	0

Leading Kickoff Returners	No.	Yards	Avg.	TDs
AFC				
Lewis, S.D.	23	578	25.1	1
Martin, N.E.-Ind.	20	483	24.2	0
Warren, Sea.	35	795	22.6	0
Williams, K.C.	24	524	21.8	0
Vaughn, N.E.	34	717	21.1	1
Mathis, Jets	29	599	20.7	0
Edwards, Buff.	31	623	20.1	1
Woodson, Pitt.	44	880	20.0	0
Elder, S.D.	27	535	19.8	0
Pinkett, Hou.	26	508	19.5	0
NFC				
Gray, Det.	36	929	25.8	0
Wright, Dall.	21	514	24.5	1
Wilson, G.B.	23	522	22.7	1
D. Carter, S.F.	37	839	22.7	1
Sanders, Atl.	26	576	22.2	1
Nelson, Minn.	31	682	22.0	0
Meggett, Giants	25	514	20.6	0
Mitchell, Wash.	29	583	20.1	0
Turner, Rams	24	457	19.0	0
G. Anderson, T.B.	34	643	18.9	0

1992
NFL Schedule

Sunday, September 6
Cleveland at Indianapolis
Detroit at Chicago
L.A. Rams at Buffalo
Minnesota at Green Bay
New Orleans at Phil.
N.Y. Jets at Atlanta
Pittsburgh at Houston
Cincinnati at Seattle
Kansas City at San Diego
New England at Miami
Phoenix at Tampa Bay
San Fran. at N.Y. Giants
L.A. Raiders at Denver

Monday, September 7
Washington at Dallas

Sunday, September 13
Atlanta at Washington
Chicago at New Orleans
Dallas at N.Y. Giants
Green Bay at Tampa Bay
L.A. Raiders at Cincinnati
Minnesota at Detroit
Seattle at Kansas City
Buffalo at San Francisco
Houston at Indianapolis
New England at L.A. Rams
N.Y. Jets at Pittsburgh
San Diego at Denver
Philadelphia at Phoenix

Monday, September 14
Miami at Cleveland

Sunday, September 20
Cincinnati at Green Bay
Denver at Philadelphia
Kansas City at Houston
New Orleans at Atlanta
San Fran. at N.Y. Jets
Seattle at New England
Tampa Bay at Minnesota
Cleveland at L.A. Raiders
Detroit at Washington
L.A. Rams at Miami
Phoenix at Dallas
Pittsburgh at San Diego
Indianapolis at Buffalo

Monday, September 21
N.Y. Giants at Chicago

Sunday, September 27
Atlanta at Chicago
Buffalo at New England
Denver at Cleveland
San Diego at Houston
Tampa Bay at Detroit
Minnesota at Cincinnati
Miami at Seattle
N.Y. Jets at L.A. Rams
Pittsburgh at Green Bay
San Fran. at New Orleans

Monday, September 28
L.A. Raiders at Kan. City

Sunday, October 4
Chicago at Minnesota
Green Bay at Atlanta
Indianap. at Tampa Bay
Miami at Buffalo
New Orleans at Detroit
Kansas City at Denver
L.A. Rams at San Fran.
N.Y. Giants at L.A. Raiders
Seattle at San Diego
Washington at Phoenix
New England at N.Y. Jets

Monday, October 5
Dallas at Philadelphia

Sunday, October 11
Atlanta at Miami
Buffalo at L.A. Raiders
Phil. at Kansas City
Phoenix at N.Y. Giants
Pittsburgh at Cleveland
San Fran. at New England
Seattle at Dallas
Houston at Cincinnati
N.Y. Jets at Indianapolis
L.A. Rams at New Orleans

Monday, October 12
Denver at Washington

Thursday, October 15
Detroit at Minnesota

Sunday, October 18
Green Bay at Cleveland
Kansas City at Dallas
Phil. at Washington
San Diego at Indianapolis
Tampa Bay at Chicago
Atlanta at San Franicsco
Houston at Denver

L.A. Raiders at Seattle
New Orleans at Phoenix
N.Y. Giants at L.A. Rams

Monday, October 19
Cincinnati at Pittsburgh

Sunday, October 25
Chicago at Green Bay
Cincinnati at Houston
Detroit at Tampa Bay
Phoenix at Philadelphia
Seattle at N.Y. Giants
Washington at Minnesota
Cleveland at New England
Dallas at L.A. Raiders
Denver at San Diego
Indianapolis at Miami
Pittsburgh at Kansas City

Monday, October 26
Buffalo at N.Y. Jets

Sunday, November 1
Green Bay at Detroit
Houston at Pittsburgh
L.A. Rams at Atlanta
Miami at N.Y. Jets
New England at Buffalo
Tampa Bay at New Orl.
Indianap. at San Diego
Cleveland at Cincinnati
Philadelphia at Dallas
San Francisco at Phoenix
N.Y. Giants at Washington

Monday, November 2
Minnesota at Chicago

Sunday, November 8
Cleveland at Houston
Dallas at Detroit

Green Bay at N.Y. Giants
L.A. Raiders at Phil.
Miami at Indianap.
Minnesota at Tampa Bay
New Orleans at New Eng.
N.Y. Jets at Denver
Phoenix at L.A. Rams
Pittsburgh at Buffalo
San Diego at Kansas City
Washington at Seattle
Cincinnati at Chicago

Monday, November 9
San Francisco at Atlanta

Sunday, November 15
Cincinnati at N.Y. Jets
Detroit at Pittsburgh
Houston at Minnesota
L.A. Rams at Dallas
New England at Indianap.
Phil. vs. Green Bay
   at Milwaukee
Phoenix at Atlanta
San Diego at Cleveland
Wash. at Kansas City
Chicago at Tampa Bay
New Orleans at San Fran.
Seattle at L.A. Raiders
N.Y. Giants at Denver

Monday, November 16
Buffalo at Miami

Sunday, November 22
Atlanta at Buffalo
Cleveland at Minnesota
Detroit at Cincinnati
Green Bay at Chicago
Houston at Miami
Phil. at N.Y. Giants
Indianap. at Pittsburgh

Dallas at Phoenix
Denver at L.A. Raiders
N.Y. Jets at New England
San Fran. at L.A. Rams
Tampa Bay at San Diego
Kansas City at Seattle

Monday, November 18
Wash. at New Orleans

Thursday, November 26
Houston at Detroit
N.Y. Giants at Dallas

Sunday, November 29
Chicago at Cleveland
Kansas City at N.Y. Jets
Miami at New Orleans
New England at Atlanta
Phoenix at Washington
Pittsburgh at Cincinnati
Tampa Bay vs. Green Bay
   at Milwaukee
Buffalo at Indianapolis
Minnesota at L.A. Rams
Philadelphia at San Fran.
L.A. Raiders at San Diego

Monday, November 30
Denver at Seattle

Thursday, December 3
Atlanta at New Orleans

Sunday, December 6
Cincinnati at Cleveland
Detroit vs. Green Bay
   at Milwaukee
Indianap. at New England
Seattle at Pittsburgh
Minnesota at Philadelphia
N.Y. Jets at Buffalo

Dallas at Denver
Kan. City at L.A. Raiders
Miami at San Francisco
San Diego at Phoenix
Washington at N.Y. Giants
L.A. Rams at Tampa Bay

Monday, December 7
Chicago at Houston

Saturday, December 12
Denver at Buffalo
N.Y. Giants at Phoenix

Sunday, December 13
Atlanta at Tampa Bay
Cleveland at Detroit
Dallas at Washington
Indianapolis at N.Y. Jets
Pittsburgh at Chicago
San Fran. at Minnesota
New Eng. at Kansas City
Cincinnati at San Diego
New Orleans at L.A. Rams
Philadelphia at Seattle
Green Bay at Houston

Monday, December 14
L.A. Raiders at Miami

Saturday, December 19
Tampa Bay at San Francisco
Kansas City at N.Y. Giants

Sunday, December 20
Buffalo at New Orleans
Houston at Cleveland
L.A. Rams at Green Bay
Minnesota at Pittsburgh
New England at Cincinnati
Wash. at Philadelphia
Phoenix at Indianapolis
Chicago at Detroit
San Diego at L.A. Raiders
Seattle at Denver
N.Y. Jets at Miami

Monday, December 21
Dallas at Atlanta

Saturday, December 26
L.A. Raiders at Wash.
New Orleans at N.Y. Jets

Sunday, December 27
Cleveland at Pittsburgh
Denver at Kansas City
Green Bay at Minnesota
Indianap. at Cincinnati
Miami at New England
N.Y. Giants at Phil.
Atlanta at L.A. Rams
Chicago at Dallas
San Diego at Seattle
Tampa Bay at Phoenix
Buffalo at Houston

Monday, December 28
Detroit at San Francisco

BRUCE WEBER PICKS
HOW THEY'LL FINISH IN 1992

AFC East
1. Buffalo
2. N.Y. Jets
3. New England
4. Miami
5. Indianapolis

AFC Central
1. Houston
2. Cleveland
3. Pittsburgh
4. Cincinnati

AFC West
1. Kansas City
2. L.A. Raiders
3. Denver
4. San Diego
5. Seattle

NFC East
1. Philadelphia
2. Washington
3. Dallas
4. N.Y. Giants
5. Phoenix

NFC Central
1. Chicago
2. Detroit
3. Tampa Bay
4. Minnesota
5. Green Bay

NFC West
1. Atlanta
2. San Francisco
3. New Orleans
4. L.A. Rams

Wild Cards: N.Y. Jets, L.A. Raiders, Denver; San Francisco, Washington, Dallas

AFC Champions: Kansas City
NFC Champions: Philadelphia
Super Bowl Champions: Philadelphia

YOU PICK
HOW THEY'LL FINISH IN 1992

AFC East

1.
2.
3.
4.
5.

AFC Central

1.
2.
3.
4.

AFC West

1.
2.
3.
4.
5.

NFC East

1.
2.
3.
4.
5.

NFC Central

1.
2.
3.
4.
5.

NFC West

1.
2.
3.
4.

Wild Cards:

AFC Champions:

NFC Champions:

Super Bowl Champions: